D0778113

WORKPLACE WELLNESS

Performance with a Purpose

Achieving Health Dividends for
Employers and Employees

Rose K. Gantner, Ed.D., NCC

Well Works
PUBLISHING, LLC

*E*ach chapter is full of research, current thinking, relevant strategies and questions to ask to ensure successful application.

—SANDRA CAFFO
Senior Director
LifeSolutions

*T*his excellent book provides the vital information needed by every organization to develop wellness programs and enhance healthy lifestyles for their employees and their families.

—DAVID MC CLURE
VP Operations
Camden Clark Medical Center

*N*ever before has it been more important for the U.S. worker to be at a high level of health, both physically and mentally. Congratulations to Dr. Gantner for writing a text that will be of such great value in improving the health and productivity of our eighty million adults who go to work each day.

—JERRY NOYCE
President and CEO
HERO-The Health Enhancement Research Organization

Well Works Publishing, LLC
1551 Staunton Drive
Moon Township, PA 15108

rosegantner@aol.com

1 2 3 4 5 6 7 8 9 10

DEDICATION

*For all who work to improve the
health and well-being of people everywhere.*

Contents

PREFACE

Purpose found me early in life. In my twenties I left a university teaching position to serve two tours of duty in South Vietnam with the American Red Cross. All day my volunteer colleagues and I were in the field with soldiers enjoying downtime so they could interact with Americans who appreciated what they were doing.

But at night we young ladies frequently visited the hospital wards at the base camps. Some soldiers were wounded in ways that were easy to see, but I always gravitated to those in the psychiatric ward whose symptoms weren't as evident. Few people talked about these soldiers because in those days mental illness came with a negative stigma.

When I returned to the United States, I earned my doctoral degree in counseling psychology and founded and directed the Center for Life Coping Skills, where the priorities were privacy, respect, and warmth. There I treated soldiers who suffered from Post-Traumatic Stress Disorder and their families as well as people with marriage and family issues.

My health care career led me into several positions of corporate power, but I never forgot those left behind in a busy, competitive world. They are my purpose and there are now too many of them, both soldiers and civilians, who suffer without help.

According to the World Health Organization depression is becoming one of the biggest and most costly health problems globally. On average, it costs up to five thousand dollars per person per year to treat depression in the United States. These days the U.S. government and U.S. Army are proactive in embracing and employing the techniques of positive psychology —a concept formed in 1998 by Martin Seligman, psychologist and researcher. Seligman's team developed a Global Assessment Tool that has been given to more than 1.5 million Army personnel. It flags and fights depressive symptoms, reduces anxiety and health costs, and, most essentially, teaches soldiers and their families to cultivate positive emotions that help them flourish.

It's time now for American businesses to become just as proactive when it comes to stress, anxiety, depression, addictions, and many other preventable, treatable conditions. If the country is to enjoy economic growth and excel in innovation, it first needs to take care of its most precious resource — people. Though improving the health of Americans and the U.S. health care system requires collaborative effort, the workplace inarguably is a huge stakeholder. It's where employees spend 25% of their lifetimes. In fact, Americans spend up to half their waking lives at their jobs or commuting to and from them.[1]

These days employees and employers in the United States are paying dearly for rising health care costs resulting mostly from conditions and life-threatening diseases triggered or aggravated by physical inactivity, obesity, and unhealthy habits people can modify. Employees pay monetarily through higher insurance premiums, steeper deductibles, and larger copays. Worst of all, they can pay with reduced quality of life and shortened life spans. Employers pay indirectly through lost productivity. Overall, health care expenditures comprise about 18% of Gross Domestic Product (GDP) and are estimated to reach 19.8% by 2020.

So it makes sense to use the workplace as an avenue to motivate employees to change unhealthy behaviors. Employees can and do become more self-directed and empowered when their employers make healthy choices the easiest choices.

This book raises awareness about how critical it is to have an emotional heart, compassion, and a positive attitude in addition to a strong, logical mind when dealing with people in and out of the workforce. *Workplace Wellness* emphasizes the acronym **HEART**:

H — **Health** to cultivate healthy habits

E — **Engagement** to optimize and sustain behavior changes

A — **Action** to take small steps

R — **Resilience** to stay connected to life purpose and passion

T — **Teamwork** to achieve maximum success and remain competitive in global markets.

Workplace Wellness is a guide for business leaders, managers, and consultants who want to decrease health care costs even as they improve employee productivity, satisfaction, and health conditions. In these pages they'll learn how to marshal some of the best practices, emerging trends, tools, and financial opportunities out there to create quality wellness and health management programs. They also will understand how the digital culture is changing the landscape of business, consumerism, and the workplace.

While *Workplace Wellness* is chock-full of strategies, tips, and testimonials, it also presents evidence. I offer statistics and facts about the economic benefits of health care, psychology, and wellness — facts to convince the highest C-suite leaders and all levels of management to buy in and be supportive.

My hope is that all my readers will end by championing this proposition: **Integrated, comprehensive wellness and employee health management programs are good business strategies.** The goals of such programs are to empower employees to accept responsibility for personal health issues they can manage, and to encourage employers to make it easy for employees to make these sensible, healthy life choices. Thus, employees can stay actively engaged in the workplace and contribute to their company's innovations, products, and profits.

Good health to all.

ROSE K. GANTNER, EdD
Pittsburgh, Pennsylvania

INTRODUCTION

A few years ago, *The New England Journal of Medicine* published a study that raised an alarm: Today's children may be the first in American history to have a shorter life span than their parents due to the health-related impact of obesity.

In the past two decades the rate of pediatric obesity has climbed dramatically, foreshadowing serious implications for the American workforce of the future. Concern is escalating about the impact of the growing percentage of the population that will be afflicted with chronic diseases at earlier ages. Increased rates of chronic disease correlate with higher rates of disability, lower productivity, and greater healthcare expenditures.

While these concerns portend the future, they surface in the current context of cost problems in the United States, which spends more than twice as much on healthcare as the next highest spending nation. Yet Americans have a lower life expectancy and poorer health outcomes on key indices than many of their industrialized counterparts.

Employers are well acquainted with the problem of the rising cost of healthcare and most recognize its relationship to chronic disease. Many, however, are unfamiliar with the extent to which lifestyle plays a role. Obesity, along with inactivity, smoking, poor nutrition, excessive alcohol use, and high stress contribute significantly to the development and management of chronic illness.

Many factors influence a person's health status, including genetic predisposition, social and cultural realities, and access to medical care and preventive services. But there is evidence that modifying attitudes about health, changing health behaviors, and providing health incentives can play a major role in preventing and managing clinical conditions such as Type 2 diabetes.

The employer-based health insurance system in the United States, through which a large percentage of the population accesses health insurance, gives employers a huge stake in controlling health expenditures for their employees. Additionally, employees are gaining additional financial incentive to control costs as they assume a growing percentage of the expense. Many progressive employers have engaged their employees in health improvement programs to improve the health status of their workforce, bend the cost curve for employee health benefits, and impact other expenses such as workers' compensation, disability, and unscheduled leave.

"Health and Productivity" has become a mantra for many employers, and innovative programs to align financial incentives with health behavior change are growing. Rose Gantner's *Workplace Wellness: Performance with a Purpose* provides a framework to better understand the business case for workplace wellness programs and the important elements needed to develop a successful approach.

I had the pleasure of recruiting Dr. Gantner in 2006 to UPMC, a large integrated healthcare delivery and financing system affiliated with the University of Pittsburgh. At the time UPMC was launching the MyHealth program to provide a set of strategies, including benefit design incentives and clinical and workplace support programs, to improve the health status of our employees and reduce the cost of group health and other health-related benefits. It was a multi-year, multi-pronged strategy. With deep industry knowledge and tremendous energy and purpose, Dr. Gantner helped develop and steer this successful UPMC program, which has resulted in major improvements in the risk profile of our fifty-four thousand employees. In doing so, the program has significantly outperformed the industry in controlling costs in group health and related leave programs.

Dr. Gantner brings that same know-how and passion to this book, which offers a wide range of strategies and a large number of examples from some of the nation's most highly successful employer programs. Also in these pages are inspiring stories of people who were able to find the right motivation to exercise, change their nutritional patterns, lose weight, stop smoking, adhere to medication regimes, and seek appropriate care. The types of workplace cultures and programs that facilitated their success also are defined.

The insights, options, and case examples Dr. Gantner provides are drawn from a diverse set of businesses and a broad set of programs. In all instances she highlights evidence-based methods that result in the kind of positive culture change and positive behavior change that mitigate health risk.

There is no "one size fits all" in this book. Rather, there is a description of a set of principles and core requirements, all based on industry best practice, that successful programs share. I know firsthand that these principles, mixed with passion, continue to help us on our journey at UPMC to grow a culture of health and deliver great outcomes.

For those thinking about how to begin a program or strengthen an existing one, this book is a must read.

Workplace Wellness: Performance with a Purpose is a valuable resource for building a road map to a healthier and more engaged workforce. Here wellness professionals will find tools to help them address the costs, the culture, and the broader strategies they need to succeed.

DIANE HOLDER
Executive Vice President, UPMC
President and CEO, UPMC *Health Plan*

WORKPLACE WELLNESS:
Performance with a Purpose

Chapter 1:

LINKING EMPLOYEE AND
CORPORATE HEALTH

The U.S. spends ninety-five cents of
every health care dollar on the treatment of illness,
and only five cents on prevention.

Everyone realizes that the national epidemics of physical inactivity and obesity jeopardize the health of employees and companies. Corporate executives, human resource managers, benefits specialists, wellness professionals, and insurance brokers are all discovering that 75% of all health care spending in the United States can be traced to obesity, physical inactivity, smoking, alcohol consumption, poor diet, insufficient sleep, poor stress management, lack of health screening, and inadequate standard-of-care management.

This massive $1.5 trillion health care expenditure doesn't include the cost of treating Americans harmed by unpredictable accidents or genetically inherited diseases or ailments. It treats the symptoms of chronic but perfectly predictable, preventable diseases – diabetes, coronary artery disease, hypertension, heart failure, hyperlipidemia, chronic kidney disease, and some types of cancer, anxiety, and depression.

The Centers for Medicare and Medicaid Services reports the United States spends ninety-five cents of every health care dollar on the treatment of illness, and only five cents on prevention, according to Gary Lindsay, director of business partnerships for Partnership for Prevention. If health care costs are to be contained, this equation needs to significantly change. Employers can spearhead that change with assistance from their health insurers and/or partnerships with wellness company vendors and professional non-profit organizations.

Committing to comprehensive wellness and health management programs that are fully integrated into a company's daily operations to drive employee participation is the socially responsible stance for companies to take.

Technologically driven tools — user-friendly web portals, links, personalized messaging, and smartphones with social network platforms — are the fastest growing ways to engage employees. Major program components should use these tools to raise awareness about self-management, biometric screenings, health assessments, fairs, health coaching, nutritional guidance, exercise, tobacco cessation, stress management, workplace competition campaigns, and condition management programs. The results can be remarkable and support lasting quality of life changes that positively affect employees, their families, their communities, and the bottom line of their employers.

$ 10,000 PER EMPLOYEE

Providing health care benefits is a huge responsibility for American employers. Costs average about $10,000 per employee and are increasing annually. If employers expand and strengthen existing programs and invest more human capital in comprehensive health management programs, while

SUCCESS GALLERY

Mikita King

HEALTH ACHIEVEMENT:
LOST THIRTY-ONE POUNDS

EMPLOYER:
BLUE CROSS AND BLUE
SHIELD OF ALABAMA

JOB TITLE:
SYSTEMS ANALYST

I was tired of seeing myself the way I was. I felt tired and sluggish. My clothes were tight, and I didn't want to go up another size.

After participating twice in Scale Back Alabama, a statewide weight-loss program promoted at Blue Cross, and not reaching my ten-pound weight-loss goal, I decided to give it one last try in 2010.

I lost five pounds. My skin was better, and my clothes fit better. Two things motivated me to keep going — my progress and the team-based approach that Scale Back Alabama takes. Some teammates exercised together, and we motivated each other.

By changing my diet and exercising daily, I was able to meet the ten-pound goal. I kept going, participating in other wellness activities at Blue Cross, such as WalkingWorks® and the Fitness Challenge. I ate more vegetables, less meat, and chose fruit instead of unhealthy snacks. Every day I limited myself to one diet drink and drank more water. I also stopped eating meals late in the evening.

Thanks to these changes, I've lost thirty-one pounds from the beginning of 2010 through the summer of 2011.

My ultimate goal is to lose an additional twenty pounds so I'm stepping up my activity level a notch. I am using the workout equipment and attending exercise classes in the Blue Cross Fitness Center, and running outside. Variety is important to me.

Having the ability to exercise at work means I don't have an excuse not to exercise.

providing a safe and trusting environment, they can convince employees to pay attention to their health and change unhealthy behavior. They can:

- Help healthy employees stay that way
- Keep other employees' conditions from getting worse
- Create a supportive and enjoyable work environment
- Improve employee recruitment and retention
- Raise employee morale
- Reduce health care costs
- Decrease absenteeism due to sick leave, disability claims, and workers' compensation
- Decrease presenteeism, a term used to describe employees who perform below par at work due to health issues
- Sharpen worker focus and engagement

- Enhance workplace safety and lessen the odds of on-site accidents

- Increase worker longevity

- Improve productivity and innovation

- Leverage social psychology and peer motivation to improve and sustain behaviors

- Reduce the social services burden on local, state, and national economies

Current research shows medical costs in the Unites States decrease by $3.27 for every dollar spent in good wellness programs, and absenteeism falls by $2.73 for every dollar spent.[2] A meta-analysis of forty-two evaluation studies of different corporate programs conducted in 2005 by Larry Chapman, health promotion author, found workplace wellness initiatives reduced absenteeism, health care use, disability claims, and workers' compensation claims by more than 25% each.

Research by Towers Watson in a 2009/2010 report showed companies with the most effective health and productivity programs achieved 11% more revenue per employee, delivered 28% higher shareholder returns, and had lower medical costs and fewer absences per employee.

In November 2010 Mercer Consulting released the results of its National Survey of Employee-Sponsored Health Plans, which included twenty-eight hundred employers. It found that for the last two consecutive years, medical costs were approximately 2% lower among employers with extensive health management programs compared with companies that did not offer such programs. Employers reported improved employee health risks and lower use rates for health services. Two–thirds of the companies are satisfied with their Return On Investment (ROI).

Researcher Ron Goetzel, PhD, and others have written about companies whose findings have appeared in peer review journals. For instance, a nine-year study by Johnson & Johnson, reported in the March 2011 edition of Health Affairs, showed a savings of $225.00 per employee per year. Additionally, Citibank over the years has spent $1.1 million on health management programs but saved $8.9 million.

Pitney Bowes was able to keep costs flat with a comprehensive integrated health management program that helps people manage health risks, reduces pharmacy expenses, and offers more low-cost drugs for chronic diseases. Together, these features have resulted in $40 million in savings over the last nine years, including a reduction in disability days for employees with diabetes and a 6% reduction in total medical costs.

Lastly, for the past four years Safeway has had flat health care costs when most other companies have seen an increase of 40% over the same time period. Part of Safeway's success is due to offering incentives to both employees and family members. If a family does not exhibit signs or symptoms of four leading chronic conditions, the employee receives a discount on his premium, saving as much as $1,560.00. Individuals can save up to $780.00.

A healthy, engaged, thriving workforce is essential to maximize business performance, remain competitive in the global market, and drive the sustainable growth of new products as well as profit. Since employers contribute about 75% of health care coverage for their employees, they should be more assertive in setting precise expectations for their employees.

THE RIGHT INCENTIVES

But convincing employees to stay healthy by changing unhealthy habits can be challenging. Efforts are sometimes met with resistance, especially if employees don't trust management, feel leaders haven't effectively communicated with them, or haven't seen their managers maintaining or improving their own health. Some employees simply go through the steps required to get an incentive their company may offer: this practice often leads to temporarily modifying behaviors rather than sustainable changes.

If incentives are to work effectively, they must be timely and person-centered; offer choices; and develop over a program's continuum of time. For example, it's best to start with an extrinsic reward to inspire participation, and over time move to progress-based outcomes, full outcomes, and social incentives. Finally, intrinsic incentives may be introduced for lasting, sustainable behavior changes.

The overall goal must be to ensure employees understand the benefits of wellness programs and actively participate in a cooperative and collaborative partnership with their managers and employers. Effective wellness and health management programs convince employees to buy into prevention by promoting the right interventions with the right information and the right incentives.

Wellness programs need to be tailored to the demographic and lifestyle characteristics of each company's culture, employees, and community. No cookie-cutter model exists.

Now is the perfect time for employers of all sizes to offer integrated programs for wellness and employee health management. Yet we know some employers and senior leaders still feel skeptical about expanding or implementing

7

comprehensive, integrated programs. Why? Many times employers don't trust the data results, or they feel the data only applies to large companies. Other times, companies lack the resources to offer incentives: the average incentive per employee is about $375.00 per year.

Some leaders have asked, "Will this integrated program really work for our company, our industry and our demographics to reduce costs? How do people change behaviors? Does proof exist that employees can be more productive and engaged in the workplace while reducing absenteeism and presenteeism?"

The answer is *yes*, but only if specific components exist, if there's quality data to support measurable outcomes, and if all responsible parties work together. Here are thirteen useful questions to ask:

1. Do the programs and services offered reflect national clinical guidelines with best practices?

2. Are the elements of the plan built into the company's policies and procedures?

3. Does the company reflect a positive culture of health?

4. Does senior leadership share the vision, align company goals and objectives, and commit staff and budget resources?

5. Are multi-year strategies in place, such as a creative, person-centric incentive plan that engages employees, adult dependents, and families?

6. Have a majority of employees had a health assessment and biometric screenings to stratify the company's population into low-, moderate-, and high-risk categories?

7. Are health coaching services available for employees and adult spouses who want to lose weight, quit smoking, reduce stress, manage their diabetes, or get Employee Assistance Program (EAP) help for anxiety or a family or relationship issue?

8. Are the programs and services communicated and promoted to employees in a personalized and targeted manner based on their readiness to change behaviors and delivered in the media such individuals prefer?

9. Is a staff member designated as the wellness manager, and is there an active wellness committee with a clear mission, vision, and annual operational plan and budget?

10. Do the programs include interventions that measure their outcomes and ways to improve as years go by?

11. Does the plan, provider or vendor offer a best practice dashboard such as the popular Health Enhancement Research Organization's scorecard? Is that dashboard shared and discussed with the employer group?

12. Do the vendor and employer share the scorecard performance results with managers and employees so everyone can understand how the results impact the company's total population?

13. Is the vendor's program accredited and has it won awards from a national organization such as the Wellness Council of America (WELCOA), The Health Project of C. Everett Koop, or the National Business Group on Health (NBGH)?

A RIPPLE EFFECT

Poor health is a serious individual, business, and economic threat to our well-being and quality of life. Yet all of us want an enhanced quality of life and extended years to live, learn, work, play, and fulfill our dreams. Moreover, we want to live with purpose, not only to be the best we can at whatever we do, but to help others and make the world better for the generations that follow. In psychological terms, this phenomenon is called "prosocial motivation," defined as the desire to protect and promote the well-being of others. Research supports prosocial motivation strengthens intrinsic motivation and strongly predicts persistence and productivity in the workplace.

Good health is about such vital goals. It's not just about regular checkups, dental cleanings, flu shots, and exercise classes. It's about the very fiber of the environment in a society's homes, schools, parks, neighborhoods, and organizations.

Since 1948 the World Health Organization has defined health as a state of complete physical, mental, and social well-being — not just the absence of disease or infirmity. WHO further defines wellness "as the process of enabling people to increase control over their health and its determinants." The WHO global model for action diagram shows how the workplace can become a central command center that positively affects many aspects of an employee's life.

The model illustrates why it's important that individuals, along with the companies for which they work, aim to create and sustain health: The influence of one employee ripples out to his community. WHO bases its call for employers to be socially conscientious about wellness on three principles. The first is business ethics: wellness initiatives are the right thing to do. The second is the business case: they are the smart thing to do. The third is the legal case: they are the legal thing to do.

Seventy percent of health is the result of lifestyle behavior choices and environmental factors. These two factors are far more critical than genetic predisposition and access to health care, which account for thirty percent.[3] **So at the end of day making better health decisions makes people healthier.**

WHO MODEL FOR ACTION: WORKPLACE ROLE IN HEALTH

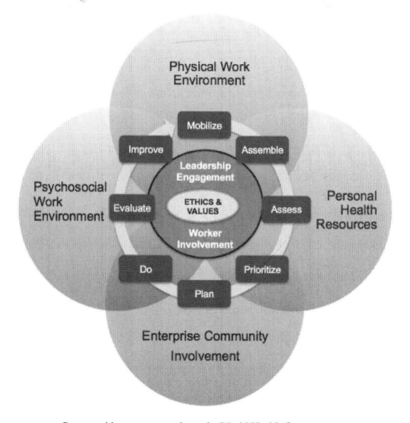

Reprinted by permission from the World Health Organization

There certainly are many decisions to make, as demonstrated in *America's Plan for Better Health and Wellness*, released by the National Prevention Council in June 2011.

Just having insurance won't make anyone healthier. Spending money won't necessarily help, either. Spiraling health care costs in the United States are unsustainable. American health care spending reached $2.4 trillion in 2008 and will exceed $4 trillion by 2018,[4] with 30%-35% of this spending considered "wasteful" or "inefficient."[5]

NATIONAL PREVENTION STRATEGY
AMERICA'S PLAN FOR BETTER HEALTH AND WELLNESS

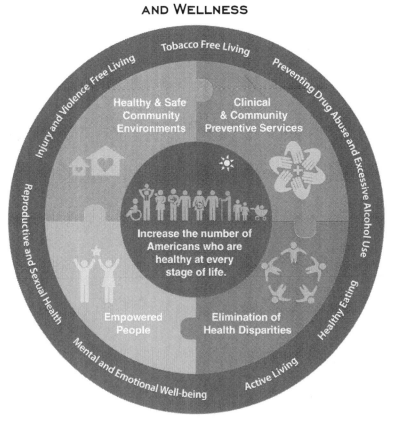

Reprinted by permission from the National Prevention Council

We need workplace wellness programs that help people understand their health as well as monitor it and make good decisions to improve it. In the American workplace, the professionals charged with improving the delivery, implementation, and evaluation of such programs and services are usually Human Resources (HR) and wellness leaders. Especially in small and midsize companies, the HR person also may assume the role of the wellness professional. A 2010 Virgin HealthMiles survey of four hundred twenty-four American companies with more than five hundred employees confirms that both employees and CFOs count on HR leaders to find the best solutions for the health care challenge. In turn, HR leaders frequently count on benefits specialists to guide them.

The January 2011 American Hospital Association report survey, including eight hundred seventy-six hospitals, showed that the HR department role in most settings is to align the design of wellness programs and policies with the company's mission. The overarching goal is to foster a supportive environment and promote opportunities for employees and families to get involved in bettering their health. If these elements are not present or not supported by senior leaders, most programs will be fragmented, weak, and result at best in offering a health assessment, biometric screening, and perhaps a physical campaign. But to stop so short is shortsighted and will not yield the participation rates, ongoing engagement, measurable results, or expectations that high-performing companies want.

This book is designed to help health professionals forge productive partnerships and build an economic case for workplace wellness programs to present to senior and middle management. An array of innovative tools, strategies, studies, examples, and end-of-chapter questions are offered as well. Professionals are invited to choose among them and fashion a wellness program that uniquely promotes the health of their companies, employees, and families.

In *Zero Trends*[6] Dee Edington, PhD, a University of Michigan researcher, lists two key challenges: "keep healthy people healthy" and "don't let people get worse."

But additional challenges need in-depth attention: recruiting and retaining talented employees, addressing psychosocial issues, improving worker satisfaction, optimizing the environment, and creating healthier communities. That's workplace wellness with a big purpose!

BUILD YOUR BEST WELLNESS AND HEALTH MANAGEMENT PROGRAM

Answer these questions as they relate to your company:

1. Whose responsibility is it at your company to create a focus on maintaining and/or improving health and well-being?

2. What programs and services are covered under total health management at your company? Are these adequate?

3. Has your company stratified its employees into low-, moderate-, and high-risk health categories? If not, what prevents this assessment from happening?

4. How does your senior management lend support for wellness initiatives and what is the next actionable step you can take to start or improve your health management program?

5. How are safety, quality, and wellness initiatives aligned with your company's strategic goals and objectives?

Chapter 2:

THE BUSINESS CASE FOR
INTEGRATED WELLNESS PROGRAMS

Measurement is at the core of
any successful business partnership.

Forty-two percent of CEOs are shifting their thinking to focus more intently on long-term planning.[7] When it comes to wellness programs, C-suite executives (Chief Executive Officers, Chief Financial Officers, and Chief Operating Officers) start by saying, "Show me the value proposition — business case and ROI."

Although leaders are investing more in wellness and health management programs, health professionals must ensure leaders understand that such initiatives can drive a business strategy by enhancing employees' performance and abilities. Best practice requires planning sessions with key leaders who agree on the strategic vision, delivery, a wellness purpose statement (operational plan), yearly targets (goals, objectives, and outcomes), robust integrated analytics, a multi-term vendor commitment, and a designated budget with adequate resources.

Now, let's list what a business case does. It answers probing questions regarding the who, what, when, where, and why of a specific proposal. It spells out how the plan corresponds to the overall market as well as the strategic vision, goals, and objectives of the company.

Generally, a business case includes an executive summary, current research, description of developmental plans and ideas, market competition, SWOT analysis (strengths, weaknesses, opportunities and threats), value proposition, developmental approach, list of resources needed, timelines, projected costs, revenue assumptions, critical success factors, conclusions, and recommendations.

For a wellness program, a business case should propose to evaluate the risk factors in a company's employed population and prioritize them based on risk prevalence, participants' readiness to change, and the cost of their impact on productivity. Key to this presentation is comparing the state of a company's employee population to the entire commercial book of business of the health insurer or wellness company.

The Medical Expenditure Panel Survey (MEPS) database provides a standardized assessment with multiple charts showing each chronic condition in the United States. To learn more, visit http://www.meps.ahrq.gov .

Chronic diseases, for instance, account for the most prevalent and costly health problems and take a heavy toll on businesses, budgets, and employees' lives.[8] Generally, the top five cost drivers in several companies are cancer, coronary artery disease, obesity, depression, and back pain (musculoskeletal).

According to the federal government, chronic diseases such as heart disease, cancer, and diabetes are responsible for seven of ten deaths among Americans each year and account for 75% of the nation's annual health spending. It is estimated 50% of all cancers are preventable. It's also important to know that the Healthy People 2010 and Healthy People 2020 initiatives sponsored by the U.S. Department of Health and Human Services, along with the new national dietary guidelines,

SPECIFIC LIFESTYLE TARGETS
Healthy People, National Standards, and Insurer's Total Book of Business

TOBACCO	TARGETS (GOALS
Healthy People 2010	12%
Current National Standard	21%
Healthy People 2020	12%
Your Organization	____
Insurer's Book of Business	____

WEIGHT MANAGEMENT	% OF PEOPLE AGED 20+ YEARS WHO ARE OBESE
Healthy People 2010	15%
Current National Standard	34%
Healthy People 2020	31%
Your Organization	____
Insurer's Book of Business	____

Calories consumed must equal calories expected for a person to maintain the same body weight.

PHYSICAL	TARGETS (GOALS
Healthy People 2010	50%
Current National Standard	44%
Healthy People 2020	48%
Your Organization	____
Insurer's Book of Business	____

POOR NUTRITION *(Under-consuming in one or more healthy food groups; or empty calories)*	% OF ADULTS
Nationwide	80-95%
Your Organization	____
Insurer's Book of Business	____

See dietary guidelines for Americans 2010: http://www.dietaryguidelines.gov

Source: U.S. Department of Health and Human Services

have set national goals to reduce both lifestyle and chronic conditions. Healthy People 2020 reflects a vision of society where all people live longer, healthier lives. It contains forty-two topic areas and one thousand two hundred objectives. For information about the Healthy People Consortium Toolkit, do visit http://healthypeople.gov/2020/consortium/hpConsortium.aspx .

Here are examples of illnesses and the costs associated with them gleaned from the National Institutes of Health, American Heart Association, and U.S. Department of Health and Human Services:

- **Cardiovascular diseases** – The world's largest killers, these diseases claim 17.1 million lives a year. Tobacco use, an unhealthy diet, physical inactivity, and harmful use of alcohol increase the risk for heart attacks and strokes. Estimated annual medical costs: $274 billion.

- **Diabetes** – Ninety-one percent of diabetes is due to poor nutrition and lack of physical exercise, not family medical history. The rate of Type 2 diabetes is expected to double in the next twenty-five years, largely as a result of people overeating. The Centers for Disease Control and Prevention estimate that twenty-four million Americans have diabetes, and that fifty-seven million more are pre-diabetic and unaware of the growing threat to their health. A total of 20% of health care expenditures go to diabetes, according to the American Diabetes Association, with the cost rising about 9% per year. Estimated annual medical costs: $174 billion.

- ■ **Chronic Obstructive Pulmonary Disease (COPD)**
  – In all, 12.1 million Americans were diagnosed
  with COPD in 2007 though twenty-four million
  were impacted, indicating the condition is
  underdiagnosed. In all, 80%-90% of COPD cases
  are due to smoking. Workdays lost per year on
  average are twelve for short-term disability, sixteen
  for absence, and sixteen for presenteeism.

PSYCHOSOCIAL FACTORS

Four of the ten leading causes of disability are behavior
disorders, which can be as debilitating as any physical illness.
The statistics from the National Institute of Mental Health,
the World Health Organization, and the book *Population Health:
Creating a Culture of Wellness*, tell the story:

- ■ Depression, the leading cause of disability, costs $58
  billion in direct costs and $193 billion in indirect
  costs per year.

- ■ Depression leads to more absenteeism than any other
  physical disease.

- ■ Depression affects 121 million people worldwide,
  and fewer than 25% of those worldwide have access
  to effective treatment.

- ■ Nearly twice as many American women as men are
  affected by depression.

- ■ 75% of mental illness starts at age twenty-four.

- ■ Combined, depression and anxiety affect 20% of the
  population.

- Alcohol and drugs kill more than one hundred
  thousand people per year.

We must dispel the stigma of behavioral health issues through open discussion and reinforce the importance of offering and using services through Employee Assistance Programs (EAP). A need exists to educate and train supervisors to identify early signs and symptoms and provide employees and families support in a safe, trusting, and confidential manner. Additionally, EAP services can include consultation with managers on a variety of topics, including managing stress, becoming more resilient, aiding disengaged workers, coping with layoffs, managing crises, and resolving conflicts. With a proper communication plan EAPs can and should be a valuable resource and cross-referral in supporting wellness programs.

LIFESTYLE FACTORS

Review these lifestyle choices and compelling facts from the Centers for Disease Control and Prevention and the American Lung Association[9]:

1. **Tobacco Cessation** — Twenty-one percent of American adults smoke, a habit that costs $167.5 billion dollars a year — $75.5 billion in health care costs and $92 billion in productivity losses from premature death. Annually, an employee who smokes costs an employer thirty-five hundred dollars more than one who doesn't. Over a lifetime, a smoker costs an employer anywhere from fifteen thousand dollars to seventeen thousand dollars more per year on average. Unfortunately, four hundred forty-three

thousand lives are lost to tobacco annually. But the good news is that 70% of smokers want to quit and 40% of them try to do so yearly.

The rate of success for smokers who use tobacco quit lines is two to three times higher than that of smokers who try to quit without assistance.[10]

For every dollar spent on smoking cessation programs, the average ROI is $1.23, according to an American Lung Association study. This study also involved Penn State University researchers.[11]

Do review the tobacco cost calculators available through America's Health Insurance Plans and the Center for Health Research, Kaiser Permanente Tobacco, at http://www.businesscaseroi.org .

2. **Physical Inactivity and Obesity** — Research shows physical inactivity and poor nutrition combine to form the second leading cause of preventable deaths in the United States.[12] They cost three hundred billion dollars in health care costs per year, with obesity alone carrying an annual price tag of $73.1 billion.

Yet with as little as a 5%-7% reduction in weight, individuals who are overweight can significantly reduce weight-related health risks like diabetes, coronary heart disease and stroke, according to the Weight Control Information Network, part of the National Institute of Diabetes and Digestive and Kidney Diseases.

A report released by the National Bureau of Economic Research in October 2010 reveals that obesity accounts for nearly 17% of U.S. medical costs — almost twice previous estimates — and adds about twenty-eight hundred dollars to a person's annual medical bills. Approximately 67% of Americans are either overweight or obese, and nearly 17% of children and adolescents from age two to nineteen.

Two reports from the U.S. National Center for Health Statistics show obesity rates have increased from 1988 to 1994 and from 2005 to 2008 in adults at all income and education levels.[13]

Weight management is about balancing the number of calories eaten against the number burned through activity. What these figures mean for the workplace is clear: employees need to move more rather than sit for long, extended periods. Remember, expanding waistlines equate to expanding psychological and physical costs for the individual and financial costs for the organization.

Often exercise is offered as the best way to improve well-being, with the prescription of walking ten thousand steps — or five miles — per day, or taking daily, brisk, thirty-minute walks at about one hundred steps per minute. Unfortunately 40% of Americans don't get adequate levels of moderate exercise (one hundred fifty minutes per week) and the average American takes only five thousand steps per day, according to the International Association for Worksite Health Promotion and the American College of Sports Medicine.

Exercise actually promotes a physical restructuring of the brain and helps neurons thrive and branch again. When we exercise, we not only learn better but develop better neural patterns for coping strategies, and that's very helpful in dropping weight. The other direct drivers of obesity are emotional health, financial stress, and lack of recognition at work.

3. **Stress** — Stress alone costs three hundred billion dollars annually, including lost productivity, workers' compensation, and leaves of absence.[14]

   Most health experts agree 75%-90% of visits to primary care physicians are for stress-related complaints, according to the American Institute of Stress. Health care expenditures are nearly 50% greater for employees who have high levels of stress. Further, employees who need to take stress-related absences from work tend to average twenty or more days away from work every year than their more mellow counterparts.

   A 2009 study from Work Options suggests 72% of employees tend to find their jobs stressful and more than 50% have trouble with managing daily stress. The American Psychological Association had Harris Interactive conduct an online survey of 1,546 adults in the United States in January and February of 2011. It found many employees feel undervalued and are dissatisfied with aspects of their job. Thirty-six percent experience stress at work regularly and 49% said low salary has a significant impact on their perceptions. Only two-thirds of employees reported being motivated to do their best at work.

   Stress also may have some hidden business costs, such as increased workers' compensation claims, increased employee accidents and injuries, and decreased customer service.

a. Financial stress is leading to illnesses such as migraines, back pain, anxiety, depression, insomnia, ulcers, weight gain, and heart attacks.[15]

b. Negative stress, called distress, raises the levels of cortisol chemicals in the body and disrupts good chemicals, namely, serotonin, norepinephrine, and dopamine.

c. Negative stress can impact worker productivity and influence others.

4. **Health Management Presenteeism and Absenteeism** – Health Management Presenteeism and Absenteeism represent major hidden costs that often are misunderstood or overlooked. The result is that employers experience several consequences, according to David Nash, MD, and others, in *Population Health: Creating a Culture of Wellness.*[16] These are:

a. Average productivity loss: one hundred fifteen hours per employee per year as a result of illness

b. Absenteeism: ten days per employee per year with a chronic illness

c. Avoidable sick days: 0.40 avoidable sick days per employee per year

d. Estimated annual cost of lost productivity as a result of absenteeism: more than $153 billion

Behind all the above statistics are human beings who can learn to change their habits and hopefully want to maintain or improve their health. We need to help employees and their families change unhealthy behaviors one step at a

SUCCESS GALLERY

Lys Severtson

HEALTH ACHIEVEMENT:
CONTROLLING STRESS

EMPLOYER:
HEALTHWAYS, TENNESSEE

JOB TITLE:
SENIOR RESEARCH AND
PARTNER SERVICES
MANAGER

I'm someone that people look at and say, "You're healthy." I'm slim, I exercise, and I eat well. But last year Healthways incorporated the Well-Being Assessment into its employee Move to Health program. The assessment measures overall well-being instead of just physical health.

When my results identified depression and high stress as areas of concern, I was shocked and thought, *That's not me.*

In the past I would have assumed that excessive stress was just a part of work life, but it doesn't have to be that way. You can be productive if you can learn to let go of stress. It doesn't matter if you're dealing with physical health issues or not. You may have that part of your life together, but mental and emotional health issues, and how you're dealing with the stress in life, have a significant influence on your health as well.

I told my supervisor I'd like to work on some interpersonal skills and how to manage the stress levels around my job. She was able to offer resources and made me feel like my request for assistance in managing work-related stress was normal.

I have a manager who is in touch and receptive. She believes her team's overall well-being is an essential component in improving our performance.

I'm still seeing a counselor occasionally. But I'm also taking steps recommended in my well-being plan that don't require medical intervention, such as making sure that I spend time with friends and family.

Everyone has to deal with stress, but it is possible to learn how to manage it in productive ways that don't keep you up at night.

time and create a healthy culture where both employees and organizations can thrive. The goal, of course, is employees who are empowered and accountable. Managing, shaping, and creating a healthy culture is a leadership competency.

Besides the business case, employers want to know how much money they will have to spend to realize cost savings. They also want to know how vendors measure outcomes and how data and results will be used to move employees to take action and affect the whole employee population.

ROI CALCULATORS AND FINDINGS

The World Economic Forum and The Boston Consulting Group have developed a new tool to evaluate a potential ROI using the 2010 Healthways Community Wellness App. In approximately ninety seconds the app can estimate the interplay among risk factors, chronic illnesses, and specific interventions, along with a five-year projection of health care costs and potential productivity savings.[17]

Estimating your organization's specific productivity losses (absenteeism and presenteeism) is a useful way to introduce the need to include health-related "indirect costs" into any discussion about the overall health of the employees and the company. Other assessments with cost calculators include several developed by the CDC[18] as well as the Blueprint for Health.[19] The latter provides a close approximation of actual productivity loss based on several characteristics of a workforce.

A January 2011 American Hospital Association report looked at health and wellness for hospital employees and found 93% of hospitals struggle to measure ROI. Those that have effectively measured show positive results. Currently, 49% of hospitals are only collecting data necessary to measure overall direct health care costs. Only 23% are looking at health care costs for specific subpopulations. In all, 23% are studying metrics on absenteeism while 8% are tracking the effects of presenteeism.

Leaders need to ensure a multi-year commitment to the process in order to thoroughly understand impacts and outcomes and set into motion continuous quality improvements. They also should share the "hard" and "soft" ROI numbers to show how poor health choices are more expensive for both employees and employers, and get everyone's buy-in. (See Wellness and Health Productivity Multi-Year Strategies chart in Appendix C.)

With proper commitment to measurement and evaluation, a significant return is not theoretical or rare. Researchers following the wellness efforts of a Midwest utility company over nine years found that while the company spent $7.3 million for its program, it ultimately saved $12.1 million in medical and pharmacy costs, employee time off, and workers' compensation costs. According to Dee Edington, PhD, University of Michigan researcher, the study shows a sustainable, well-planned program will provide savings.[20] Further research by well-respected pioneers in the field, such as Larry Chapman, MPH, of the Chapman Institute and Ron Goetzel, PhD, of Emory University, indicate modifying lifestyle risk factors realizes savings in four major areas: short-term disability, medical and pharmacy costs, absenteeism, and workers' compensation. Moreover, other associated productivity costs can be up to two-thirds greater than direct medical expenditures.

Unfortunately, most companies lack an integrated, systematic approach when it comes to calculating ROI and committing to wellness programs. But the companies who do enjoy significant payoffs. Although admittedly not easy, the task is doable. In a survey conducted by the National Business Group on Health[21] two-thirds of survey respondents stated the biggest worksite challenges in the United States are:

- Employees' poor health habits

- Employees' poor attitude

- Employees' lack of participation in a wellness program

The opportunity to improve these conditions in the workplace lies significantly with the C-suite leaders. Judd Allen's study[22] shows only 5%-10% of this group are "wellness champions," or active believers. He found 30%-40% are quiet supporters; 40%-50% neutral; 15%-20% quietly opposed, and 1%-2% actively opposed. Imagine encouraging even a small percentage of these leaders toward positive change. Such an effort not only would promote a productive work environment but create committed "champion ambassadors" to keep employees actively engaged in changing harmful behaviors. The whole time health risks — and their associated costs — would decrease. All parties could make great strides.

Adults are most likely to change in healthful ways when they are supported by friends and family and when they enjoy an inviting work culture, solid benefits, incentives, and company policies backed by opportunities to improve health initiatives. Research supports the assertion that up to 75% of all lifestyle risk factors (smoking, weight management, nutrition, physical activity, stress management) are modifiable. So it behooves all of us in the health industry and business community to continually find creative ways to keep employees and family members actively engaged in improving their habits, attitudes, and lifestyle and, by extension, lowering their risk factors.

The ideal is to have at least 75% of any employee population in the low-risk category. A low-risk employee has zero to two risk factors, for example, a smoker with high blood pressure. A moderate-risk employee has three to four risk factors, for example, a smoker with high blood pressure and asthma. Lastly, a high-risk employee has five to six risk factors.

Generally, research supports that a low-risk employee costs less than one thousand dollars per person per year, while one at moderate risk costs up to forty-nine hundred dollars, and one at high risk costs at least five thousand dollars. Edington's[23] research indicates an average of 64% of a company's population will fall in the low-risk category, 26% in moderate risk, and 10% in high risk. These numbers will vary, depending on each company's population, industry, and demographics, as well as the wellness initiatives it implements. Ideally, the goal is to get 85% or more of a company's population participating in a health assessment, biometric screenings, health coaching and advocacy, and one to two program activities. That's a challenging goal since now most companies have below average employee participation rates, the average being 30%.

Some companies, however, have achieved and continue to accomplish these high performance goals. The UPMC System, Johnson & Johnson, and Union Pacific are good examples, as are Quest Diagnostics, American Express, General Electric, IBM, Campbell Soup Company, and Baptist Health South Florida.

THE GOVERNMENT FACTOR

The Affordable Care Act (ACA), signed into law by President Obama in March 2010, must be taken into account. It contains many provisions, which will roll out through 2014, that impact employer and employee plans positively and negatively.

On the downside, employers will have to raise the annual maximum amount that employees pay for health care costs. About 63% of large businesses anticipated that these adjustments would occur in 2011, according to a survey conducted by the National Business Group on Health that comprised seventy-two companies employing more than 3.7 million people. This same group has wisely developed for its members an information and communication tool kit to help them understand the key employer provisions in the new law.

ACA includes six provisions that directly impact wellness programs and services, according to the Health Promotion Advocates.[24] They are:

1. Development of a national health promotion plan

2. Enhanced health promotion research

3. Technical assistance to enhance evaluation of workplace health promotion groups

4. Regular periodic surveys on workplace health promotion programs

5. Grants, available for five years, to pay a portion of the cost of comprehensive workplace health promotion programs for small employers

6. Permission for small employers to offer employees a premium discount of up to 30%, and perhaps eventually 50%, for positive lifestyle practices in health promotion programs. Approximately 84%, or four million, small businesses were eligible for a tax credit on their 2010 returns for the purchase of employee health insurance. Sadly, 56% of small business owners were unaware of this tax credit.[25]

The next several years may be the best time in history for businesses to harness the help of the government in forming their own wellness programs. A word to the wise, though: some provisions may change once the Supreme Court makes a final ruling in Spring 2012 on whether ACA is constitutional.

BUILD YOUR BEST WELLNESS AND
HEALTH MANAGEMENT PROGRAM

Answer these questions as they relate to your company:

1. What are the top three lifestyle and chronic conditions identified in your employee population through a health assessment, and, more importantly, what programs or services are you offering to mitigate those risks?

2. How does your organization's scorecard compare with Healthy People 2020 initiatives and your carrier's or wellness vendor's entire book of commercial business?

3. Has your company used any of the new ROI calculators available to understand how to best impact your total population and reduce health care costs?

4. How does your company compare to other high-performing, quality companies that implemented comprehensive, integrated wellness and health management programs?

5. What is your organization's stance and actions in regard to preparing for the Affordable Care Act and, specifically, the wellness provisions it recommends?

Chapter 3

BUILDING A CULTURE OF HEALTH

Establishing new wellness norms at a steady rate of two to four per year is an essential function of a health culture.

Culture is made up of leaders and followers. A company's culture — its collective norms, rules, and expectations — often stem from its origins. The early leaders found ways of doing things and reinforced their successes. Their values became standard procedures. A company, for example, can be recognized by its eagerness for action, a preference for starting projects, or a desire to be first in the marketplace. Another company may be identified for its strategic planning, goal-setting, and analyzing. New hires in these companies will be expected to adjust their behaviors and reframe their preferences to comply with accepted norms.

THE POWER OF CULTURE

Social psychology research shows that the environment surrounding us has a compelling effect on our behavior. We need to belong. We might not realize we're aligning our behavior to fit in, but we are. To decide to be different is to make a very serious choice with possible negative consequences.

An employee also navigates a gap between what a company declares as its norms and its actual norms. A company, for instance, may say it values teamwork and then only reward individual achievement. It may state respect as a core value and then promote employees known for disrespectful behavior because they bring in new business.

But wait. There isn't just one culture in a company. There are group-based subcultures. Groups can be delineated many ways — departments and workgroups, location and geography, management and labor, IT and sales, clinicians and non-clinicians. The norms of each group create internal cultural diversity. The local experience of the culture is further shaped by managers and supervisors who have a dominant influence on the day-to-day rules and messages about behavior. Employees more actively participate in programs when their managers are trustworthy, according to Right Management, a firm specializing in designing solutions that align a company's business strategy with its talent. Such managers, who emphasize benevolence and integrity, also are more likely to share information about how employees' work benefits others and serves an important mission.

On top of these dynamics, cultural influences change. Companies move through stages of development. Technology advances. External forces require repositioning, mergers and acquisitions, layoffs and new hires. Scandals rock the company's image and assumptions. Such is a corporate landscape, and a key role of leaders is to manage and shape the culture, or set of cultures, as a business asset and a source of pride, innovation, and profitability.

Now, think of norms related to wellness topics: weight management, physical activity, stress, tobacco, and nutrition. The first step in creating a culture of health is assessing where a company currently stands in relation to the health of its employees. Is a company's culture of health positive, neutral, or negative? Take an audit. What behaviors are expected, modeled, and reinforced regarding food choices, exercise, life balance, substance use, relationship development, and attention to staying healthy? A virtual representative focus group, or members of an existing wellness committee, may be able to voice the norms and messages influencing healthy behaviors.

Judd Allen has written extensively about this topic:

> *A wellness culture features norms that make it easier for people to maintain healthy lifestyles — for example, it could be a strong norm to drink water and eat nutritious snacks low in fat, sugar, and salt. Freedom of choice would still be honored because people could bring in their own junk food and soda without being ridiculed. In another health culture example, the norm would be for employees to use their breaks for physical activity, healthy eating, stress management, and friendship; the smoking break would not be the only way to get a time out.* [26]

Allen maintains that establishing new wellness norms at a steady rate of two to four a year is an essential function of a health culture. Policies, procedures, and programs, as well as informal, unwritten social mechanisms, are used to reinforce and sustain these norms so they become embedded in daily expectations and rewards. This work is a critical and essential part of the role of HR, benefits, and wellness leaders.

That said, cultural norms and assumptions are very engrained and difficult to change. All human systems attempt to maintain equilibrium. Shared assumptions that cumulate over time provide an identity. **Doing things differently means unlearning and relearning and that's uncomfortable, even threatening, for most people. Employees are more likely to attempt behavior changes when they are invited to do so and are guided and given choices as well as a positive motivational message rather than a message of fear.**

In 2010 Edgar Schein, expert and thought leader in organizational culture and leadership, identified eight activities that must be carried out to create a climate of safety:[27]

1. Spelling out a compelling positive vision that clearly states exactly what the new way of working will be, described in specific behaviors and including why the organization will be better off

2. Offering formal training for a new skill or knowledge

3. Involving learners in managing their own learning process

4. Informally training relevant groups and teams so new norms and assumptions will be jointly built and shared

5. Practicing, coaching, and giving feedback so people know how they're doing and can learn through trial and error

6. Modeling positive roles so people can see the new behavior or attitude in others with whom they identify

7. Offering support groups in which problems can be aired, discussed, and jointly resolved

8. Forming systems and structures and leadership that support a new way of thinking and working, making the changes possible and desirable in the workplace

This process is transformative and risky. Influencers who reinforce old cultural elements can be removed, but new cultural elements will only be retained if new behaviors lead to success and satisfaction. Employees learn quickly to distrust and dismiss initiatives that represent temporary enthusiasm, little personal meaning, conflicting messages, and no benefit. They look for cultural supports around them. Are they there? It's critical that they be in place before strategic behavioral change is solicited.

The investment of company leaders across all subcultures is essential, too. Employees will look to them to set an example. They will notice the walking shoes under the managers' desks, bowls of fruit in the break rooms, circulating sign-up sheets for programs, and wellness items on team meeting agendas. They will see their managers taking the stairs and the picture of the CEO at a biometric screening. Then they just may visit the mobile health van or on-site clinic, and join in celebrating with their friends when someone meets an important health goal.

CULTURE COMES FIRST

When large U.S. employer groups were asked what factors were most pressing regarding employee performance, the answer was clear: organizational culture. **The message for building great wellness programs is that organizational culture must change before individual and interpersonal behaviors do.**

A culture of health is generally defined as an organizational climate that promotes healthy lifestyle choices. The November 2010 Buck Consultants global survey showed only 33% of participating companies believe they have a culture of health today, though 81% intend to pursue this goal in the near future.[28] The significant gap shows that the culture of health is perceived as something to work toward achieving. In 2011 Buck Consultants found that despite the fact that American employers spent more money on employee wellness programs in 2010, only 37% of them measure their program's effectiveness.

Like commercial employer groups, the American Hospital Association (AHA) survey results reported in January 2011 confirm the need for hospitals and their employees to be leaders and serve as role models in creating a culture of health. John Bluford, chairman of the AHA board of trustees, said the mission of many hospitals is the health of their communities, which starts with the health of hospital employees and their families. AHA is implementing wellness strategies with a program entitled "A Call to Action: Creating a Culture of Health." Do visit the website http://www.aha.org/wellness for more information.

At hospitals and elsewhere, musculoskeletal and behavioral health problems show up as paramount in affecting employee performance. In 2009 the World Health Organization predicted that in a few years stress and depression will be the biggest issues in the workplace around the globe. According to Buck Consultants, stress already is identified as the foremost health factor in most countries. To get ahead of this trend, companies need to integrate their Employee Assistance Programs (EAP) with their health strategies and put more emphasis on training staff, including leaders and managers, as well as line staff on resiliency, optimism, happiness, mindfulness, and change management.

The September 2010 edition of *Pointer View*, an Army civilian newsletter, contains startling facts about depression and suicide. From the invasion of Afghanistan in 2001 through the summer of 2009, eight hundred seventeen soldiers killed themselves, compared to seven hundred sixty-one who were killed in action in Afghanistan. Probably because many soldiers feel reluctance and fear of reprisal if they seek professional counseling and medication, the Army launched a campaign called "Shoulder to Shoulder: I Will Never Quit on Life." Its mission is to offset a growing trend among Army veterans and service members who contemplate or attempt suicide.

In its campaign the Army emphasizes that maintaining an active, healthy lifestyle leads to a healthy mindset. In recognizing and accepting this significant challenge, the Army displays resiliency and determination. We'd all do well to follow its example.

DYSFUNCTIONAL CULTURES

Recent research confirms the association between high job pressure and cardiovascular disease, metabolic syndrome, depression, exhaustion, anxiety, and weight gain. According to researcher Diana Fernandez, MD, it's time to create corporate policies that better protect the health of workers.[29]

The Center for Work-Life Policy,[30] a New York City think tank to be called the Center for Talent Innovation starting in 2012, found that over the past twenty-five years employee workloads have increased, mainly due to technological advances and more intense, competitive work environments where the mantra is "do more work with fewer employees." This pressure is felt by blue-collar workers all the way up to the boardroom and, over the past decade, has led to more workplace violence, absenteeism, and workers' compensation claims.

SUCCESS GALLERY

Linda Wallace

HEALTH ACHIEVEMENT:
LOST THIRTY-FIVE POUNDS

EMPLOYER:
SPRINT, KANSAS

JOB TITLE:
BENEFITS ANALYST

Over the last couple of years, I have wanted to improve my health and wellness. To get started, I turned to several resources offered by my employer.

First I took a free personal health assessment through Sprint's wellness program. Then I took advantage of a free twenty-eight-day trial offered by Sprint's on-site fitness center in Overland Park, Kansas, which ultimately led to joining the low-cost fitness center.

After participating in a weight-management program through the center, a fun weight-loss competition with co-workers, and a corporate fitness challenge, I'm pleased to say I am more than halfway toward my goal of losing sixty-five pounds.

In the midst of life's ups and downs, celebrations, successes, griefs, and disappointments, stress hands me emotional challenges. My support system and wellness coaches, as well as what I've learned from the various programs. in which I've participated, all help me face these challenges head-on.

Throughout this process my motto is to "live life." Eliminating foods or not celebrating an event is not an option for me; the real change for me has been exercising moderation in my choices and lifestyle.

My very supportive family, along with a workplace that encourages health and wellness, help make my journey successful. My doctors also are pleased with my results and expect that by the time I reach my goal, my medications for blood pressure and asthma will be reduced.

The Gallup-Healthways Well-Being Index offers many more insights into stress, work, happiness, and health. For instance, people who are not engaged in their work, or who don't get to use their strengths daily, experience more stress and anxiety. Also, employees who have a best friend in the workplace — only 31% of respondents did — are seven times more likely to be engaged and enjoy their work environment. For those without a best friend in the workplace, the odds for engagement and enjoyment dropped to one in twelve. Do visit the index website, http://www.well-beingindex.com .

In *Wellbeing: The Five Essential Elements*, Tom Rath and Jim Harter[31] write about their study, conducted in one hundred fifty countries and covering 90% of the world's population. Their findings reveal five universal, interdependent elements of well-being that shape all our lives: professional, social, financial, physical, and communal. While 66% of people are doing well in at least one area, only 7% are thriving in all five.

We need to do much better in the workplace. Talented people leave work environments, voluntarily or involuntarily, when they know their supervisors don't share their values, demonstrate an emotional heart, or show any interest in their personal growth. Unfortunately, too many supervisors, under tremendous pressures to increase productivity and profits, sometimes lose perspective and forget that a project takes combined talents and that no one person can successfully perform all the multi-functions alone. Or supervisors stick to unrealistic timelines, forgetting some projects are held up until other responsible parties complete their portion.

Research shows that 52% of absences occur on Mondays and Fridays, that several employees unexpectedly take off the day after a big football game, and that the most productive days of the work week are Tuesday and Wednesday.[32] As managers and leaders, it's good to know the most productive days and when, perhaps, to inquire about project updates.

With more focus on wellness programs that emphasize lifestyle and psychosocial health, in addition to medical aspects, hope exists that bright and talented people with kind souls and good hearts can use applied research to change work dynamics for the better. Everyone would prefer having and being around productive employees who are satisfied, happy, resilient, and healthy.

THE WORK/LIFE BALANCE

According to a study by researchers at Harvard and McGill universities,[33] the United States lags far behind nearly all wealthy countries when it comes to family-oriented workplace policies such as maternity leave, paid sick days, and support for breastfeeding.

"More countries are providing the workplace protections that millions of Americans can only dream of," said Jody Heymann, MD, PhD, founder of the Harvard-based Project on Global Working Families and director of McGill's Institute for Health and Social Policy.

"The United States has been a proud leader in adopting laws that provide for equal opportunity and diversity in the workplace," she added, "but our work family protections are among the worst." The study notes the United States is one of only five countries out of one hundred seventy-three that doesn't guarantee some form of paid maternity leave.

Also, American workers average approximately ten paid holidays per year while British workers average twenty-five holidays and German workers, thirty, according to Heymann. When all work hours are tallied, Americans work twelve weeks more per year than Europeans do.

Unfortunately, in June 2010 the House of Representatives voted down The Work-Life Balance Award Act (H.R. 4855),[34] a bill that would have established an annual Work-Life Balance Award that the Secretary of Labor would bestow annually on employers with exemplary work-life policies. The vote dismayed representatives from the Equal Employment Opportunity Commission, Society for Human Resource Management (SHRM), and the National Partnership for Women and Families.

These groups noted that many legislators don't understand the importance of the bill and issued a statement: "Encouraging workplaces to develop these policies goes to the heart of how we value our nation's families and our economic competitiveness. Employers that recognize the value of helping their employees achieve a work-life balance should be recognized and copied." They're right. **Genuine work/life balance is a practice, not a slogan.**

On a positive note, in early 2011 the Society for Human Resource Management and the Families and Work Institute launched a new partnership called Moving Work Forward.

Its mission is to increase the number of employers who use flexible workplace arrangements. The partnership will develop educational materials and practical tools to help employers and HR personnel advocate for and implement effective workplace strategies. According to a SHRM survey, 58% of employers said workplace flexibility is the most effective way to recruit and retain top talent, even more effective than compensation.[35] Deloitte LLP, a company that embraces this policy, consistently has been ranked among the best places to work by *Fortune* and *Business Week*. It also has earned a number of Alfred P. Sloan Awards for Business Excellence in Workplace Flexibility.

For several years the American Psychological Association (APA)[36] has awarded organizations of all types in the United States and Canada for programs and policies that foster employee health and well-being and enhance organizational performance. The Psychologically Healthy Workplace Awards are given at the state and national levels. Nominees are evaluated on their workplace practices in the following areas:

- Employee involvement
- Health and safety
- Employee growth and development
- Work-life balance
- Employee recognition

Company winners for 2011 include Cross, Gunter, Witherspoon & Galchus, a law firm (Arizona); eXude Benefits Group (Pennsylvania); San Jorge Children's Hospital (Puerto Rico); and Kaiser Permanente Center for Health Research (Oregon). Do visit the website, http://www.phwa.org , for more details.

Stopping bullying in the workplace also is good for business. Some employers realize that anti-bullying policies promote a culture of health and accountability. The Sioux City Community School District in Iowa is the first in the nation to address bullying for its adult employees.

Bullying can take many forms, including verbal abuse and offensive conduct that threatens, humiliates, intimidates, or interferes with work. Some workplace bullies intentionally sabotage other employees and their work performance. The problem, prevalent among 37% of American adults, contributes to employee disempowerment, lack of self-esteem, disengagement from the workplace, and the stress-related complications of anxiety, depression, and hypertension. Bullying should be replaced with interpersonal behaviors that demonstrate respect, ethics, integrity, cooperation, collaboration, and teamwork, all hallmarks of a civil workplace culture.

The United States, however, is last among the Western democracies to adopt a law forbidding bully behavior in the workplace. Most European countries and Canada have laws compelling employers to prevent or correct bullying. Laws are needed because employers react to them with policies. Gary Namie, director of the Healthy Workplace Campaign, and Daniel Yamada, professor at Suffolk University Law School, have drafted the Healthy Workplace Bill. The virtual headquarters for this anti-bullying bill, one of the boldest proposed changes to U.S. employment law in forty years, is at http://www.healthyworkplacebill.org .

In addition to important work in the worlds of law and policy, health cultures will continue to evolve in workplaces of the future. A confluence of technological advances has made it easier to minimize the need to be physically present in an office space or even work from 8 a.m. to 5 p.m. But the changing nature of work isn't limited to the notions of time and place.

Relationships between employees extend across time zones and the globe, and require better technologies to create effective work environments.[37] Most interesting is the way social media, electronic collaboration on work documents, cloud-based storage services, and touch-based tablets have migrated from personal to professional use. The iPhone, iPad, Skype, and video conferencing improve communications, collaborations, and interdisciplinary teamwork even as they force new policies. Certainly these technologies also easily integrate freelancers into the work process and facilitate job sharing.

It's no wonder that in recent years many business leaders have changed their attitudes and now believe working remotely helps worker productivity. Forty-two of the top fifty small to midsize companies that won Best Places to Work Awards in 2011 support flexible work hours and more virtual offices.

BUILD YOUR BEST WELLNESS AND HEALTH MANAGEMENT PROGRAM

Answer these questions as they relate to your company:

1. In your organization is the overall culture of health positive, neutral, or negative?

2. What policies and opportunities has your organization created to promote active employee and family engagement for those with group health coverage?

3. How would you rate the perception among your leaders and managers regarding work/life balance and, most importantly, do you think your employees and line staff would agree with this rating?

4. How has the nature of work changed in your organization and what percentage of employees work from home or other virtual areas?

5. How does your organization actively involve employees who are in remote locations or virtual offices to participate in your company's wellness programs and services?

Chapter 4:

STRATEGIES AND INTERVENTIONS FOR SUCCESSFUL BEHAVIOR CHANGE

People can learn, unlearn, and relearn
new behaviors anytime — if they choose to do so.

Creating a comprehensive corporate wellness program requires directing three types of healthy change in the workplace: personal, interpersonal, and organizational.

At the base of all change is human behavior and motivation as they are scientifically understood. In recent years, behavior economics, neuroscience, and positive psychology all have helped explain how a human being changes. Grounded in evidence-based science that supports the interplay of the body, brain, and healthy lifestyles, these fields are playing active roles in the design of worksite wellness programs.

When people consider behavior change they are internally evaluating the following questions: What's in it for me? Do I believe I can make this change successfully? Am I ready to change? What are others around me doing? Answers to all these questions are key in creating behavior change, which is a type of navigation. We need to know where we are and where we want to go. The following steps usually are necessary:

- Setting and committing to a small goal

- Having a strategy for the goal attainment

- Paying attention and focusing in the moment

- Having energy and optimal vitality to follow through with plans

BJ Fogg's[38] lab research on behavior design and technology from Stanford University is especially exciting. Fogg's team has developed a behavior grid model that shows fifteen ways behavior can change and incorporates an easy-to-use behavior wizard tool for thinking about behaviors and persuasive technologies. His research shows three elements must converge at the same moment for a behavior to occur: motivation, ability, and triggers that activate habits. He contends that if a particular behavior doesn't occur, at least one element was missing.

Key concepts from Fogg's lab trace how behavior changes:

- Dot behavior: take an easy step.

- Span behavior: do the behavior for forty days.

- Path behavior: integrate the new habit so it becomes a life change.

But all paths must start with a dot, a small step. For example, a sedentary person who wants to exercise daily may start by stretching for a few minutes daily. Ultimately, this simple activity leads to behavior change. To learn more, visit http://www.BehaviorModel.org .

Wellness companies and health insurers are taking notice. Healthways and Humana, early adopters in wellness programs, are using such research to enhance their current programs.

THE BRAIN AND CHANGE

It's generally accepted that behaviors are reflexive, or driven by habit. Kevin Ochsner, the founding father of social neuroscience, contends humans are guided by habits 70%-80% of the time and by deliberate reflective thought only 10%-30% of the time.[39]

Often humans live on autopilot and make quick choices without realizing their long-term consequences. The key to making good choices frequently is to learn how habits are formed in the brain.

Though it weighs about 2.7 pounds, the brain contains one hundred billion neurons and is highly adaptable throughout a person's life because the hippocampus, or memory center, retains the ability to form new neurons to assist in growth and learning. It takes only one neuron to form a new memory. This concept supports that people can change behaviors at any age, if they choose to do so.

Kelly Traver, MD,[40] author of *The Program: The Brain-Smart Approach to the Healthiest You ~ The Life-Changing 12-Week Method*, writes the brain wants to continue whatever is normal and maintain a balance called homeostasis. The hypothalamus, or brain center, is the master of homeostasis and controls hunger, thirst, and body temperature. It also determines a person's stress response.

Any change that occurs too rapidly or suddenly causes the brain to resist, according to Traver. A brain's resistance pattern plays a major role when a person wants to adopt a healthier lifestyle. If a person is asked to make a big change, the amygdala, or stress response center, activates. If a person is asked to make small changes, however, the amygdala remains quiet.

This biological fact illustrates why good wellness programs emphasize gradual, incremental changes in addition to learning new stress responses. By practicing new actions time and again, a person essentially outsmarts his own brain into readjusting and creating a new norm. The process takes patience, attention, and lots of positive feedback. For example, if a person has a bad habit that needs changing, it's best to start with a positive statement, such as: "You are really good at that. Now, we want you to develop a new skill, which is required in our company and culture."

INTERPERSONAL BOOSTS

Adult learning relationships begin and flourish with mutual respect. If relationships are positive, friends, colleagues and teammates form a synergistic blend in which the group perceives itself as better able to achieve goals as a unit than any one member would alone. The focus becomes "we" and "us" winning together. Certainly the whole team wins when engaged in healthy relationships that improve each player's well-being.

The workplace itself can be optimized as a social network to boost the success of every individual employee, much like Weight Watchers encourage one another by social modeling and acknowledging small successes.

John Dewey, American philosopher and psychologist, stressed that education and learning are social, interactive processes. He also emphasized the importance of learning by doing. So a workplace wellness committee may create social opportunities for employees, for example, a weight race campaign with teams. A team may meet three times a week in the cafeteria to share updates on progress, eat yogurt, drink low-sodium V8 juice, enjoy an apple as a quick lunch, and use the rest of the time to walk together for thirty minutes. The camaraderie that develops could lead to after-work softball teams or shared workout times at a local gym.

Besides the websites of insurance carriers, popular sites that do an amazing job with social networks, peer-to-peer support, and daily campaigns are Shape Up, http://www.shapeup.com , specializing in physical activity campaigns; SparkPeople, http://www.sparkpeople.com ; and Me You Health, http://www.meyouhealth.com . On these sites people share and exchange information and stories, read and respond to blogs, and learn new ideas from each other on how to modify unhealthy behaviors.

American workplaces are now embracing the principle of "do, learn, and change" because they need self-motivated, self- managed learners. Our companies are places of constant change that require constant learning. A case in point is IDEO, a design and innovation consulting firm. Under Chris Waugh's leadership, IDEO employees brainstorm with customers to come up with solutions. They start with the phrase "How might we do—" and go on to achieve results that are realistic for the workplace. They have created, for instance, easy-to-use pre-prep cooking kits for non-cooks. Some employees volunteer to use an innovative product and teach others in the workplace or home to use it, all while encouraging people to share photos of their experiences with the product and pass on the skill.

Other trends and technologies also are drastically changing informal and formal workplace learning and social interactions. Who would have imagined adults to be receptive to E-Learning? The free university website, http://www.blackboard.com , exemplifies how effectively knowledge can be shared internationally through e-courses. Many worksites offer required annual courses virtually. This kind of learning, generally defined as transferring skills and knowledge through a computer network, will continue to grow. Besides saving much of the time required to offer courses in a traditional classroom, E-learning increases access, flexibility, and speed in training sessions.

Mobile applications, known as M-Learning, are growing just as quickly due to smartphones such as the iPhone, for which there are now more than five hundred thousand applications available for downloading. Smartphones are mini-computers due to their ability to interact with Twitter, Facebook, and other platforms, and create new communities. Interactive adult gaming, or gamification, also is growing as games create step-by-step journeys, rules, challenges, competition, and rewards for improvement.

ORGANIZATIONAL REINFORCEMENTS

Of course the organization itself contains the individuals and interpersonal groups. Like a sophisticated life support system, a corporate wellness culture can facilitate and enhance all positive efforts made within it.

The Accountable Care Act will incorporate the AMSO model[41] of behavior change developed by Michael O'Donnell, PhD, founder and editor-in-chief of the *American Journal of Health Promotion*. AMSO explains how individuals raise awareness, become motivated to change, learn new skills, and avail themselves of opportunities in their environment to choose and reinforce new behaviors. The acronym stands for:

- **"A"** Awareness, valued at 5%
- **"M"** Motivation, valued at about 30%
- **"S"** Skills, valued at about 25%
- **"O"** Opportunities in the environment, valued at 40%

This model shows us education and information alone will not change behaviors. Nor will focusing on health risks. A wellness program must incorporate many strategies.

Let's use smoking cessation as a model. Everyone knows smoking is harmful. Yet one in five Americans — 20.8% — still smoke. A goal of the national health promotion plan is to reduce prevalence of cigarette smoking to 12%. The least educated and working poor have the highest smoking rates while only 12% of college graduates smoke.

Roughly 70% of American smokers want to quit, but the cycle of chemical and psychological addiction is difficult to overcome. Only 40% of smokers try to quit in a calendar year. In fact, it takes multiple attempts to finally achieve success. Just as detrimental as smoking are smokeless tobacco products such as snuff, cigars, and water pipes, which are gateways to lifelong addiction.[42]

National health policies undeniably save lives. For many years, nothing changed in American workplaces until researchers discovered secondhand smoke actually kills six hundred thousand people a year, as many as are lost in car crashes. This statistic provided the rationale for state and national smoke-free workplace policies, the Clean Air Act, and free quit clinics nationwide. In June 2009 President Obama signed into law the Family Smoking Prevention and Tobacco Control Act, which gives the U.S. Food and Drug Administration regulatory authority over tobacco products and their marketing. As of January 2010, twenty-six states and the District of Columbia have laws prohibiting smoking in all public places and workplaces, including restaurants and bars.[43]

Once carriers and/or companies decided to reduce tobacco use in the workplace, as well as the chronic conditions it causes, they gave their employees opportunities to participate in a tobacco campaign. Opportunities included health coaching, free nicotine replacement therapy (NRT) medications, and an opportunity to talk with a pharmacist on the phone about different medications. Carriers urged their physician providers to refer their smoking patients to quit programs. These combined strategies contributed significantly to reducing workplace tobacco prevalence rates. Research shows that if a person smokes and tries to quit with a NRT product, he doubles his chances of success. If he uses a NRT product and a health coach, his chances are six times greater.[44]

Union Pacific has achieved tremendous success in reducing the prevalence of smoking by applying many of the above strategies over seven years. Originally, 40% of its employees smoked. Rates fell to 25% and are now at 11%.

Some organizations go a step further. If an employee self-reports as a tobacco user and chooses not to participate in the multiple programs offered to quit, he will incur a penalty in the form of higher insurance premiums.

Other HR offices have written policies stating that new hire prospects may not apply if they smoke. This policy is now being used by Alaska Airlines, Cleveland Clinic, and Memorial Hospital in Chattanooga, Tennessee.

The tobacco campaign can be adapted to reduce other unhealthy behaviors along with other lifestyle programs.

JUST THE RIGHT INCENTIVES

Different people respond to different motivations, including self-mastery, achievement, recognition, competition, hope as opposed to fear, pleasure as opposed to pain, and social acceptance as opposed to social rejection. To try to motivate

SUCCESS GALLERY

Leroy Lee

HEALTH ACHIEVEMENT:
QUIT SMOKING

EMPLOYER:
UNILEVER, CONNECTICUT

JOB TITLE:
ASSOCIATE FINANCE
MANAGER

I've never wanted to be an old man smoking two packs of cigarettes a day and hacking his lungs up. That's a pitiful picture, isn't it?

Yet it took me so many years to quit because I was afraid to fail. My long-time friends just accepted me as a smoker, but the new friends who started coming into my life questioned my smoking. They were my motivators.

I generated my support system, which included joining Unilever's UNI*Care* Benefits of Choice program, by telling a lot of people that I was quitting. That helped because everyone was watching me to see if I could really follow through.

I quit smoking in four weeks, and there's no way I will ever smoke again.

someone interested in self-mastery with social acceptance simply won't work. Using the right incentives and offering some choices is essential for behavior change.

Carefully chosen incentives are an integral part of any comprehensive wellness program. Financial incentives, such as insurance premium reductions, cash, gifts, and raffles, can drive participation in healthy lifestyle campaigns. Approximately 50% of large companies provide these rewards for employees and 21% for dependents. The average incentive amount is $375.00, according to an October/November 2011 survey by The Parthenon Group and ShapeUp, a wellness company. The survey encompassed twenty-five large companies ranging in size from three thousand to three hundred thousand employees.

A survey conducted by the National Business Group on Health showed 68% of employees say they change behaviors because of an employer incentive plan. These days the work of HR and benefit specialists is easier to monitor and measure since incentive platforms are automated with an optional point system. Some companies are shifting the emphasis from participation to outcomes; they reward employees for small steps they achieve toward a major health goal. For example, enrolling in a program may automatically get an employee X amount of points, while completion requires X plus ten points. This approach supports linking incentives to outcomes to improve employee engagement and sustain behavior changes.[45]

As a program matures, it ideally will turn some of its external financial incentives into intrinsic and social ones that an employee inwardly values. Change efforts based on extrinsic motivations tend to fail in the long run, while outcome-based incentives and intrinsic motivations result in sustainable behavior change.

ORGANIZATIONAL CHANGES

Of course individuals and interpersonal groups are not the only things that need to change for the better. Sometimes wellness plans should, too, by way of responding, adapting, and improving.

All organizations should use vendor partners with the expertise to deliver multi-year wellness programs with specific goals as well as the means to measure how the programs are doing. A company should get: quarterly reports; a scorecard that tallies employees' participation in various activities and outcomes; completed satisfaction surveys; and statistics showing the reduced prevalence of risk factors and readiness to change among all employees.

Wellness committee members, selected from all levels within the company for their expertise, should evaluate their specific scorecards and compare their results to that of their carrier's commercial book of business. Only then can wellness programs be effectively adjusted to refocus on different risks, hold employees' interest, and reduce costs.

Additionally, a quality integrated health management program can be evaluated on how it handles leaves of absence and disability programs. **The ultimate question is this: Did your organization add value; improve the health of its employees, dependents, and family members; and save money?**

Several companies have won awards for their excellent wellness programs. (See Chapter 10.) Some include Lincoln Industries, Johnson & Johnson, Medical Mutual of Ohio, Pfizer, Volvo Group, Berkshire Health Systems, Citibank, Dow Chemical, and Lowe's.

LEGAL AWARENESS

When creating, navigating, and evaluating a wellness program, remember to respect both employees and the law. Always adhere to the Health Information Patient Protection Act (HIPPA), all privacy guidelines of the Genetic Information Nondiscrimination Act, and the Americans with Disabilities Act.

Say a company chooses to offer incentives for completing a health assessment. That assessment cannot contain any genetic information regarding family medical history. Similarly, the incentive must be available to all similarly situated individuals. Also, if it's unreasonably difficult for an individual to meet an initial standard, a reasonable alternative standard must be available to him. WellSteps offers a free tool, the Wellness Compliance Checker. Do, however, seek legal counsel in designing and implanting wellness programs to ensure compliance with all laws.

BUILD YOUR BEST WELLNESS AND HEALTH MANAGEMENT PROGRAM

Answer these questions as they relate to your company:

1. Has your organization incorporated any new and innovative scientific evidence into the design or implementation of wellness and health management programs?

2. What multi-components for health coaching does your company offer? Have you explored computer-based instant chat for your members in addition to telephonic and on-site health coaching?

3. What incentives and incentive platforms do you or your vendor provide to track and monitor members' progress?

4. Do your organization's programs consider behavior change and how such changes occur at three levels: individual, group (teams), and organizational?

5. Does your organization's program offer employees and adult dependents choices with regard to incentives and discounts or rewards?

Chapter 5:
WHAT POSITIVE PSYCHOLOGY OFFERS

Approximately 50% of large companies offer stress management programs, but many stop short of offering instruction in happiness, positivity, resiliency, or mindfulness.

Few U.S. employers realize that recent surveys show their employees are unhappy and disengaged.

Sadly, American companies don't even rank employee morale, or well-being, as priorities, according to Workplace Wellness Strategies, a November 2010 global survey by Buck Consultants that encompassed more than one thousand two hundred organizations based in forty-seven countries and representing more than thirteen million employees.[46] The top concerns of U.S. employers were found to be reducing health care costs; improving productivity and decreasing presenteeism; and reducing employee absence. But it's not like that in most of the world. The survey revealed companies in Europe, Asia, Australia, Canada, Latin America, and Africa rank improving workforce morale and engagement as the first or second top strategy in their wellness programs.

It's no wonder U.S. companies are more keenly concerned with rising health care expenditures; their foreign competitors don't bear a similar burden. But American employers still would do well to go beyond reducing risk factors for disease and employ positive psychology components to help employees be optimistic, happy, and resilient people who are sick less and produce more.

A Harvard School of Public Health study found that people who are generally optimistic are less likely to develop hypertension and other chronic conditions (2009).[47] The research further supports that positive thoughts generate positive feelings and actions. In numerous scientific studies positive emotions have been linked with better physical health, longer life, and greater well-being.

But research also shows most people are far more negative than positive in their private thoughts. Unfortunately, chronic anger, worry, resentment, and anxiety have been linked to increased risk for heart disease because people who have such emotions react to them with increased blood pressure and constricted blood vessels.

POSITIVITY AND PERFORMANCE

Our brains are hardwired to perform best when we're optimistic and positive, not negative or neutral. We can maximize our brain potential and happiness by finding meaning and purpose, which both precede professional and personal success and growth.

Scientists agree that there is a biological dimension to happiness and that the brain is the central command center for the necessary chemical and physiological changes. Researchers say the neurotransmitter dopamine activates the reward system associated with joy and desire. On the downside, dopamine also is associated with the uncontrollable urges addicts feel to repeatedly engage in behaviors that are at first pleasurable but turn destructive. Endorphins are brain chemicals that increase dopamine. We can help control both by making moderate choices. For example, if we want to eat chocolate, we can take a small piece or two instead of a whole box. If we want alcohol, we can drink a glass instead of a bottle.

More widely accepted now is the practice of training managers and employees about brain health and resiliency, and showing them how to become more hopeful and optimistic, which leads to being more productive. The foundation for such training should begin with learning and applying resilience. Gail Wagnild, PhD, researcher and senior consultant, has developed The Resilience Scale, a proactive and global tool. She also has created the Living a Resilient Life Program, which effectively aids individuals, groups (teams), and organizations.

Resilience is generally defined as the ability to adapt and bounce back after adversity. If resilience training is introduced in the workplace, the learned competency skills can prepare both employer and employees ahead of time for various risk situations, prevent the severity of stress-related disorders, and enhance peak performance. The good news is that anyone can learn to build resilience. Strengthening resilience transforms lives because it helps people make changes at a fundamental level.

The five core characteristics that are the heart of the resilience are:

- Meaningful life ("What was I born to do with meaning and passion?")

- Perseverance ("Quitting is not an option.")

- Self-Reliance ("I can do this.")

- Equanimity ("I always keep the big picture in mind.")

- Existential aloneness ("I am my own best friend.")

This material is supplemented by mutually supporting others, learning to engage life fully, and finding a balance of work/self responsibilities with time for rest and leisure activities. To learn more, do visit www.resiliencescale.com .

In short, positive psychology is about recognizing personal strengths and playing to those strengths, rather than focusing on weaknesses. It complements traditional psychology and involves intervening in healthful ways to build thriving individuals, families, and communities. Hungarian Psychology Professor Mihaly Csikszentmihalyi, one of the fathers of the movement, put it this way, "People who learn to control inner experiences will be able to determine the quality of their lives."

In 1998, Martin Seligman, a University of Pennsylvania psychologist and researcher, started a revolution in his field when he became head of the American Psychological Association. He declared psychologists need to focus attention on healthy people, not just those who suffer from behavioral issues such as depression.

In his 2002 book, *Authentic Happiness,*[48] Seligman validated that people must use many of their strengths and traits to increase their happiness. He defines happiness as a preponderance of positive effect over negative effect in an individual's thinking, and further holds that positive feelings maximize our social, intellectual, and physical abilities.

In *Flourish*, his 2011 book, Seligman writes about signature strengths such as kindness, originality, humor, optimism, and generosity, and contends people can cultivate happiness by identifying and using many of them. He even offers a Signature Strengths Survey.

Seligman's early work delineated the differences between pessimists and optimists. Pessimists, for instance, believe that bad or unpleasant events will last a long time and are their fault, according to Seligman. Pessimists also believe one mistake inevitably leads to more. On the other hand, optimists believe defeat or failure is a temporary setback and is not their fault but rather stems from events outside themselves. Being an optimist or pessimist comes down to self-talk. An optimist chooses a perspective of empowerment, and a pessimist one of disempowerment. To learn more, go to Seligman's website, http://www.authentichappiness.org, and take a self-assessment.

The main point is that optimism is a skill of emotional/ social intelligence that can be learned. Approximately 50% of large companies offer stress management programs, but many stop short of offering training and interventions regarding happiness, optimism, resiliency, or mindfulness, defined as paying attention and staying in the moment. Such interventions needn't be elaborate or expensive. For instance, practicing mindful meditation using simple breathing and relaxation exercises aids in expanding awareness, curiosity, and intuition.

Positivity, the 2009 book by Dr. Barbara Fredrickson,[49] advanced Dr. Seligman's work. A social psychologist, Fredrickson states that being more optimistic allows for greater possibilities in problem solving, and that positivity obeys a "tipping point" — a sweet spot in which a small change makes a big difference. The goal for individuals is to create those sweet spots and live daily with a ratio of three positive thoughts and actions for each negative thought. Presently, 80% of Americans fall short of this goal, but can improve and measure themselves by going to http://www.positivity.com and taking the quiz.

Most profound is that Fredrickson's research supports that positivity doesn't simply reflect success and health; it produces them. **We can conclude that success for a company is more likely if its workforce is filled with purposeful, resilient, positive people.** Examples of companies who demonstrate a happiness culture are Google, Zappos, and SAS.

Positive Organizational Scholarship is a cousin to positive psychology and offers varied approaches to scientifically investigate, process, and focus on the best of human conditions that occur within organizations. The main focus is on "positive deviance" and what is right in an organization rather than what is wrong. This methodology has proven results that support high-quality relationships and exceed organizations' goals. This approach, for instance, was used in the cleanup and closure of the Rocky Flats Nuclear Arsenal in Colorado in 2006. In "Positive Leadership: Strategies for Extraordinary Performance," Kim S. Cameron[50] writes the crew completed the project sixty years ahead of schedule, thirty billion dollars under budget, and thirteen times cleaner than required by federal standards. The work team employed positive leadership strategies, which include a positive climate, positive communications, positive relationships, and positive meaning. In essence, this crew poured their hearts, minds, and spirits into this project. Today the site is a magnificent wildlife refuge for all to enjoy.[51]

Research by Baker, Cross and Wooten[52] found that individuals can be identified as "positive energizers" or "negative energizers" and showed how this difference has major implications for individual and group performance. Positive energizers have the ability to create and support vitality in others — a learned behavior. Research supports that high-performing companies have three times more positive energizers than average organizations.

BOOSTING PRODUCTIVITY

We've all heard employers want to increase employees' productivity and decrease health care costs. Any discussion of the issue first requires a definition of "worker productivity." It's the value of goods and services produced in a period of time, divided by the hours of labor used to produce them. Productivity is reported quarterly by the Bureau of Labor Statistics at http://www.bls.gov. Investors pay attention to these reports because they know what the Federal Reserve Board knows: high productivity is the key to allowing the unemployment rate to drop to low levels without risking inflation.

But productivity suffers in workplaces characterized by criticism, lack of teamwork, and unhealthy gossip, according to a Right Management[53] poll of one thousand four hundred four human resource personnel and senior business leaders. Results showed more than 60% of organizations are suffering from negativity detrimental to productivity and performance.

These are the answers to the poll's main question: Has negativity at your workplace impacted productivity?

- 61% said yes, employees are struggling to stay focused.

- 36% said sometimes, but the issues are addressed.

- 3% said no, employees are staying positive.

Certainly employees have a duty to be responsible for their behaviors and contribute to a safe, trusting, fun environment. We all know that some instead opt to make difficult situations worse. But it's also important not to let negativity and criticism take over the workplace because it can spread like germs. As leaders, none of us can afford to allow an environment that throws anyone "under the bus," blames others for our own actions and responsibilities, or perpetuates an untrusting atmosphere where disrespect and lack of appreciation become the norm.

Good companies that want to recruit and retain talented employees — and keep them engaged — know that the behaviors and attitudes of senior leaders, managers, and HR staff establish the culture of the work environment. We have all heard the phrase, "People are your greatest assets." In fact, people are far more than statistical data that focus on absenteeism, presenteeism, retention, turnover rates, and financial profits. Yes, these are all critical components in reducing health care costs and evaluating quality, products, services, and profitable results.

But an equally important question is, "Do senior leaders and managers demonstrate emotional hearts?" In other words, do employers communicate effectively? Do employees know what's expected of them, feel valued, and have quality relationships with their supervisors? If the answer is yes, the employees in the corporate culture are likely to be engaged, confident about job security, and therefore productive.

Research supports that engaged employees enjoy better health and feel less negative stress than their disengaged counterparts. Results also indicate that disengaged employees have increased anxiety and depression and are less productive, resulting in more direct and indirect costs to the company.

According to a 2010 employee engagement study by Gallup,[54] disengaged employees erode an organization's bottom line even as they break the spirits of colleagues in the process. Many such employees have reached a point of unprecedented burnout. Within the U.S. workforce, Gallup estimates their cost to the bottom line to be more than $300 billion in lost productivity alone.

SUCCESS GALLERY

Michael Kauffman

HEALTH ACHIEVEMENT:
LOST WEIGHT

EMPLOYER:
GLAXOSMITHKLINE
BIOLOGICALS, MONTANA

JOB TITLE:
SITE CONTROLLER

I began my career with GSK in June 2007. At that time, I weighed about 245 pounds, had little concept of healthy eating, and did not exercise except for the occasional hike into the mountains. Such hikes inevitably led to exhaustion and a recovery period of several days.

My daily routine consisted of waking up just in time to shower and make it to work, which did not allow time for breakfast. By mid-morning, I was ravenous and foraged for brownies, doughnuts, or whatever I could find to hold me until lunch. Since I was starving, lunch was a grand affair with huge portions of unhealthy food.

When I arrived home, I would have a snack, followed by dinner and an evening of TV watching while eating a huge bowl of tasty ice cream or other sweet treat.

I received a jolt of reality when my daughter, Alissa, came home from college in early 2008. She hadn't seen me in several months, during which time I had further expanded in size. An aspiring doctor, she was appalled and told me I needed an immediate and substantial change.

I decided it was time to enroll in the fitness center at work, read the literature on healthy eating, read what the GSK calendar said about eating and exercise (yes, those calendars do help), and take the annual health survey.

Support structures at work and at home pushed me toward the goals I had in mind. I visualized what I might look like and how I would be able to hike without getting so tired.

Slowly, I became more physically fit, made time for breakfast (hugely important), and ate less and better quality food. At some point, our site switched cafeteria vendors to a company that prepares much healthier cuisine.

It took me more than a year to drop to a low point of 197 pounds. Since then, I have stabilized at around 205 pounds, roughly fifteen pounds over my ideal body weight. My long-term goal is to reach 190 pounds.

Since making the change, my annual health survey readings get better each year, I do not stress out easily, and I sleep better at night. I am mentally on top of my game during the day and more productive at work and home.

Being healthy positively affects nearly every aspect of my life. The wellness program has been a true game-changer.

DEGREES OF ENGAGEMENT

Gallup also framed the disengagement problem in terms of the workforce, finding 29% of U.S. workers are engaged while 56% are disengaged and 15% are actively disengaged. Considering the expensive and widespread nature of the problem of engagement, it's useful to define and evaluate it as precisely as possible. Benjamin Schneider,[55] senior research fellow at Valtera Corporation and winner of the 2009 Michael R. Losey Human Resource Research Award, defines engagement in terms of employees' feelings and behavior. An engaged employee is persistent, proactive, adaptive, and does work beyond his job description. Engagement, however, is not the same as job satisfaction and has nothing to do with getting an employee to do more work for less pay. The difference is that engaged employees are focused and passionate in how they approach their tasks and goals.

Schneider also noted that companies with high levels of satisfaction also enjoy lower absenteeism, turnover rates, and substance abuse. Interestingly, trust, fairness, autonomy, and meaningful work were found to drive employee engagement. So it behooves HR managers to assist line managers in designing positions that help employees invest in themselves and their sense of well-being. Thoughtful job descriptions are key to a workplace filled with positive employees who feel passion and purpose.

What does it really mean to treat employees fairly? Schneider found these practices constitute fair treatment:

- Distributing rewards, promotions, and bonuses
- Demonstrating respect and warmth through interpersonal relationships
- Involving people in decision-making
- Offering opportunities to question decisions

Other research on what differentiates an engaged employee from a disengaged one comes from ORC, a market research firm[56] that studied a database of seven hundred thousand records from two hundred twenty employee surveys conducted in various countries since 2008. ORC divided employees into three categories to measure how engaged they were at their jobs:

"Say" employees: "I feel proud to work for my organization," and "I would recommend their products and services."

"Stay" employees: "I feel a strong sense of belonging to the organization," and "It would take a lot for me to leave."

"Strive" employees: "This organization energizes me to go the extra mile," and "I feel motivated to do the best I can in my job."

Only 35% of respondents are classified as "ideal" employees in all three categories. While most intended to stay with their companies, almost four of ten employees do not "strive" for their employers.

Sometimes employees along a career path get marginalized and lose some of their desire and motivation because of compounded negative outcomes that build over time. They also can lose drive because of complex work environment issues, including changes in roles, supervisors, expectations, and leadership personality styles. Perhaps the main issue in all these circumstances comes back to trust, fairness, autonomy, and meaningful work and whether managers help employees understand why they're a critical part of the company's future.

Ultimately, it's the line managers who can significantly help increase employee participation with the level of trust and emotional commitment they cultivate. To enhance their motivation, employees need to observe and experience:

■ Role clarity with clear expectations of duties and responsibilities

■ Opportunity to see projects through completion and celebrate successful achievements

- Feedback on their particular role in interdisciplinary projects

- Help connecting their efforts to the bigger mission and purpose

- Acknowledgment of and respect for their work and talents

A three-year rating of U.S. cities and states, however, reveals a continued downward trend in well-being at work. In March 2011, the Gallup-Healthways Well-Being Index suggested 2010 was another hard year at the office. Specifically, the Work-Environment Index continued its descent, scoring 50.9 in 2008, 49.1 in 2009 and furthering its decline at 48.2 in 2010 and 48.0 in 2011.[57] As discontent rises in the United States, so does a lack of trust in employee/supervisor relations. **The message is clear: Talented and engaged workers want a partnership with their supervisors and managers, not an authoritarian relationship.**

Additionally, the relationship that both the company and employee have with the world is crucial for engagement. Roy Spence, founder of the Purpose Institute in Texas, has helped many companies such as Southwest Airlines, Whole Foods Market, and Wal-Mart not only achieve financial growth but use their talents to make a difference in communities nationally and globally. In his book, *It's Not What You Sell, It's What You Stand For*,[58] he writes that when a purpose is in place, employee engagement is higher, competition less threatening, and customers more loyal. With a purpose in place, positivity flows.

Purpose and passion are the secrets to developing a more fulfilled work life as well as a healthier bottom line.

BUILD YOUR BEST WELLNESS AND HEALTH MANAGEMENT PROGRAM

Answer these questions as they relate to your company:

1. What components of positive psychology would your staff find most appealing in terms of training and/or incorporating into existing wellness programs?

2. What interactive, interdisciplinary team exercise could be used to increase productivity and morale in your workplace?

3. Can you articulate to senior leaders and managers the importance of applying resilience training as opposed to stress management training, including what benefits could be derived?

4. In your workforce are there more positive energizers or negative energizers?

5. Can you suggest how your organization can re-direct focus to what is right in the organization and apply more positive leadership principles?

Chapter 6:

SATISFIED EMPLOYEES AND THE BOTTOM LINE

Some research suggests U.S. job satisfaction
is so low that 45% of employees intend to
start searching for new jobs as soon
as the economy recovers.

Eighty-four percent of employees polled in 2010 and 2011 Manpower surveys said they planned to look for a new position the following year. Only 5% said they intend to remain in their current position.

"Employees are restless and feel they are lacking in options," said Right Executive Vice President Bram Lowsky, who added that the findings are a barometer of both job commitment and worker distrust in management. "It's the workplace equivalent to whether or not the country is moving in the right direction. Sometimes called 'flight cognition' by behavioral psychologists, employees' intent to leave is far from an unusual phenomenon. When it applies to four out of five employees for two years running, however, it has to be of top concern to senior management."[59]

According to the surveys, employee complaints are numerous and include more shift work but no bonuses or pay raises. They also say that their immediate supervisors take advantage of them and demand far more work output, and that their companies don't replace employees who leave.

When even well-insured employees who are relatively well paid are unhappy, worker dissatisfaction must be acknowledged as an elephant in the room. Yet the elements that converge to make a satisfied employee are no secret: they get to make decisions and have a job with clearly defined responsibilities. Further, the ideal work environment supports open, honest communications without fear of reprisal from supervisors or being called into the office "for further clarification."

In short, the work environment of a satisfied employee is safe, diversified, friendly, professional, and collaborative. It encourages innovative ideas from all employees, no matter their position or title. Employees want managers and leaders to articulate the key message of the company, and share its vision and goals. They want to be inspired. On the other hand, employers want high performers who can increase productivity.

If both parties are to succeed, it's up to company leaders to create a sense of purpose, hope, direction, and trust. Employees deserve to know reliable facts about their company, including a truthful account of its financial health, why it's in its present state, and how it plans to continuously improve. After all, they're devoting precious life energy and talent to the company and its mission.

However, organizations globally tend to regard wellness in the workplace as an asset of little business value, according to the Society for Human Resource Management as well as a 2009 Right Management survey. Less than 49% of almost thirty thousand respondents in fifteen countries agreed with this statement: "My organization actively promotes health and well-being." In the United States, 60% agreed.

According to the Great Place to Work Institute,[60] reporting on a number of its recent studies in January 2010, U.S. job satisfaction is so low that 45% of employees intend to start searching for new jobs as soon as the economy recovers. These findings are substantially lower than those of Manpower though each study evaluated a different time period and was administered differently. No matter what the exact percentage may be, however, a large percentage of employees with that much dissatisfaction clearly can't be ignored.

Learning from the best

The Great Place to Work Institute is known for producing Fortune Magazine's 100 Best Companies to Work For® list. Through data-backed assessments, the institute also provides senior leaders and human resource personnel the ability to recruit and retain top talent by developing a workplace culture they love. Such a culture results in committed, inspired employees as well as refined HR programs and practices that maximize every dollar spent on "people" programs.

The companies that make the list of the best places to work all have embedded in their cultures a survey process from which to collect employee feedback and ideas. Voluntary turnover at these companies is two to four times lower than industry norms. For example, the health care and social assistance industry's average turnover is 17.4%, compared to 7.2% among the best hundred companies. The Great Place to Work Institute promotes something that transcends policies and practices. It isn't just what these companies are doing; it's how their leaders are doing it. Another key point is that good to excellent companies continuously improve.

Drawing on its twenty years of research, the institute defines a great work environment as a place where employees trust the people they work for, have pride in what they do, and enjoy the people they work with. Such workplaces are measured by the quality of the following three interconnected relationships:

employees and management, employees and their jobs, and employees and other employees.

Top on the list in 2011 is SAS Institute, a North Carolina company with more than five thousand employees that develops business analytics software used in virtually every industry across the globe. People continually try to decipher what magic underlies the continuous cycle of invention, creativity, and performance that makes this company so unique. **Obviously, the magic is in the mission statement: "SAS starts with the belief that we are in the business of people — whether that is with customers, employees or business contracts."** The company has interesting, innovative ways of speaking succinctly and directly with its employees:

- Executives speak directly and honestly with employees and answer their questions in one-on-one conversations and small groups.
- Several executives have internal blogs.
- Leaders do live webcasts as part of the SAS Leadership Live Program.

Like all great companies, SAS takes special care in recruiting its talent. In addition to possessing the required job skills, successful candidates must reflect the company's five values. SAS employees are expected to be approachable, swift and agile, innovative, trustworthy, and devoted to focusing on customer needs. The expectation that every employee will make a difference shows up in the company's bottom line. Founder and CEO Jim Goodnight states the company has been financially successful all thirty-four years of its existence.

SAS, which has a stellar reputation for the quality of its operations, estimates its average employee's total benefit package is equivalent to more than 40% of that employee's salary. Its employees' perception of their work environment and the opportunities created for them is well documented. The SAS turnover rate is 2.2%.

Recreational Equipment (REI), which ranked ninth on the 100 Best Companies to Work For® list in 2011, specializes in outdoor sports retail. Based in the state of Washington, it has ten thousand employees nationwide and is owned as a co-operative. REI's core purpose is to inspire, educate, and outfit for a lifetime of outdoor adventure and stewardship. Employees are granted time to volunteer to build trails, restore habitats, and work on other service projects; the company gives incentives and points for such community activities.

REI's wellness and health management goal emphasizes prevention. Its active and enjoyable wellness programs include challenges and campaigns that embrace the outdoors and nature. Even an employee who works just five hours per week receives some health care coverage. Additionally, employees can be transported to and from work and, in the event of a home emergency, are guaranteed a taxi. REI's turnover rate is minimal. In 2010 its sales were $1.66 billion, up 14% from the previous year, and its net income was $30.2 million. Of course, all employees share in the annual profits.

The Great Place to Work Institute also releases lists of Best Small and Medium Workplaces and the 25 Best Multinational

Companies to Work For. Among the best small and medium workplaces:

- 42 of 50 have flexible work schedules

- 42 of the 50 offer additional paid days off for paid maternity leave

- 23 offer on-site massage therapy

- 19 match employee charitable contributions

POWER OF THE SOCIAL NETWORK

Research supports that our well-being as adults is influenced by our network of relationships. We all tend to model and imitate those close to our inner circle of friends. What kid doesn't look up to a favorite teacher, neighbor, or family friend as a hero? What adult can't trace the positive effect of that hero through a lifetime?

Two professors made this process, called social contagion, well known in their 2010 book, *Connected: The Surprising Power of Our Social Networks and How They Shape Our Lives.*[61] Nicholas Christakis, professor at Harvard, and James Fowler, professor at the University of California, San Diego, say social contagion works like any other type of contagion — through transmission from one person to another. What's transmitted? Behaviors, norms, emotions. What you feel, think, and do is influenced even by what your friends' friends' friends feel, think, and do. Social networks are capable of spreading happiness, generosity, and love.

With regard to business, the professors report that certain positive environments foster trust and respect throughout a network and bind a group together. Negative environments, however, foster different patterns of network ties and are best only for transmitting information. This understanding helps

SUCCESS GALLERY

Lois Galligan

HEALTH ACHIEVEMENT:
DIAGNOSING AND TREATING
CANCER, SUSTAINED SUPPORT
PAST RECOVERY

EMPLOYER:
SAS, NORTH CAROLINA

JOB TITLE:
CORPORATE FINANCE
MANAGER

I experienced the advantage of the on-site SAS Health Care Center firsthand in 2009 when I made an appointment to see a doctor about edema. Based on blood test results, the doctor there recommended I proceed immediately to a hospital emergency room. At the hospital I was diagnosed with cancer.

After the diagnosis came surgery, a two-week hospital stay, and chemotherapy – none of it fun, but the SAS comprehensive medical coverage eliminated one major concern: the cost. That's only the beginning.

After my medical leave came a six-month period where my energy level was not what it had been. My team did a terrific job supporting me in both tangible ways (balancing my workload) and intangible ways (those important small gestures of kindness).

Since then, SAS has continued to support my physical, mental, and emotional well-being through:

- Personal trainer recommendations based on my special needs, and group workouts at the SAS fitness center.
- On-site services that save time and energy.
- Classes that have educated me on healthy food choices and helped me learn to meditate and improve my garden.
- Cafeterias that provide delicious, nutritious meals at great prices.
- Beautiful grounds and art-filled halls, which inspire me each day.
- I'm thankful for every day I'm here — on earth and at SAS.

us learn more about teams and teamwork within any given organization.

For example, if your best friend close to you at work quits smoking, you are 34% more likely to quit. If your best friend is overweight, the probability is you are 54% more likely to be overweight. Other health-related behaviors that might spread within a social network include the tendency to get health screenings and flu shots, visit doctors, and select a provider hospital.

The real question the authors propound is whether networks can affect our capacity to govern ourselves with honesty and achieve our goals of spreading well-being among many, not just a select few. They feel optimistic networks can be used to reduce inequality because people often ignore their selfish tendencies when interacting with people to whom they are connected.

LIVING BETTER, LIVING LONGER

The goal for many companies and individuals is the same — a long, happy, healthy life that benefits others and self.

It's unlikely, however, that any company will move forward successfully in this global economic environment with anything but satisfied, high-performance employees.

Leaders and managers who want to retain the talent that sustains and advances them simply must listen to employees and make decisions partially inspired from the bottom up, rather than exclusively from the top down. Indeed this new model will be essential for all companies that plan on surviving and thriving into the twenty-first century.

Companies that will be successful well into the future also must understand what conditions lead to sustaining a healthy, long human life because their staffs comprise human beings. The time to start working on this project is right now. While the United States leads the world in medical research and medical care, it isn't even in the top twenty-five in one of the most important health indicators — longevity.

As of this writing, the oldest person in the world is Besse Cooper of the United States, who is one hundred fifteen years old. The oldest man is Jiroemon Kimura of Japan, who is one hundred fourteen. Only 1% of the world's population becomes a centenarian. What allows them to achieve such longevity? The primary reasons probably are related to lifestyle. Evercare,[62] a company that specializes in coordinating care for senior health, commissioned a 2010 survey of seventy American women and thirty men who were at least ninety-nine years old and reported the following:

- Nearly one-third had watched a reality television show, and 27% had watched MTV or music videos. One in seven had played a video game.

- Eighty-two percent have dietary habits that stayed the same or improved over time.

- Seventy-seven percent had never smoked.

- Seventy percent live at home, either alone or with a spouse.

For more information, do reference Dr. Andrew Weil's website, http://www.drweil.com .

The survey supports other research that states centenarians are forward thinkers who are open to new experiences, generally eat healthy foods, don't smoke, have a strong religious faith, and cherish their independence. The U.S. Census Bureau reports there are eighty thousand American centenarians but estimates there will be five hundred eighty thousand by 2040. That's a sevenfold increase.

Interestingly, the so-called Nun Study has shown that quality of thinking and writing early in adult life correlates with cognitive ability and health sixty years later. Other things being equal, nuns whose writing in the 1930s showed higher "idea density" were better off physically and cognitively when they reached their nineties and lived an average of seven years longer than nuns whose writing wasn't advanced.[63]

A seventy-two-year-old Harvard University longevity study on happiness, which has tracked two hundred sixty-eight men from the 1930s, identifies seven factors that contributed to their long lives.[64] Dr. George Valliant, former director of the study, said the men:

1. Consistently and maturely adapted to changes

2. Were well educated

3. Had stable marriages

4. Exercised

5. Didn't smoke

6. Didn't abuse alcohol

7. Generally maintained a healthy weight

Also, 80% of the men served in World War II. The summary basically supports that joy and hardships happen to everyone along their life journeys, that navigating both well is important, and that having some warm connections with others is necessary and healthy for effective coping. Adapt, connect, and care: it's good advice for companies, too.

In November 2010, two very old companies merged. Chicago-based RR Donnelley and Sons Company, founded in 1864, purchased Bowne, which dated to 1776. The companies, which each had adapted to a changing world, are a good fit. Bowne, which started as a printing company, provides shareholder and market communications services. RR Donnelley and Sons, which has sixty-five thousand employees, is a global provider of integrated communications, software design and development. It works collaboratively with more than six thousand customers worldwide to develop custom communications solutions that reduce costs, enhance ROI, and ensure compliance.

Thomas J. Quinlan III, RR Donnelley's president and chief executive officer, comments on the company's website about its 2011 third-quarter performance.

"We continue to have success in the marketplace, winning new work and expanding customer relationships," Quinlan said. "Given the challenging global economic environment and sluggish financial markets activity, we are pleased with our results. Despite these headwinds, we generated more than

$300 million of operating cash flow in the quarter, an increase of over $90 million from last year's third quarter."

With regard to its employees, RR Donnelley is focused on promoting healthy choices and preventing future health problems. On-site health screenings are offered annually, and more than two thousand two hundred employees participate in the company's weight loss and maintenance program. All eligible employees can participate in a smoking cessation campaign, chronic condition campaign, and Green Step Challenge, a walking program.

According to Quinlan, RR Donnelley considers the best measure of the company's social responsibility to be the daily actions of its employees across the globe.

BUILD YOUR BEST WELLNESS AND HEALTH MANAGEMENT PROGRAM

Answer these questions as they relate to your company:

1. What actions, policies, and/or benefits should your company emulate to keep more employees actively engaged, retained, and productive in the workplace?

2. Would you vote for your company to receive a Great Place To Work Award? If so, what does your company do best?

3. Can you identify the best social networks and key managers in your organization to promote the importance of wellness and health management programs?

4. As a leader, can you ensure that employees have an opportunity to provide emotional, physical, or intellectual support to others in addition to receiving support from others?

5. Can you articulate your company's mission statement?

Chapter 7:

COLLABORATIONS ARE KEY
TO THE FUTURE

*Some health plans and wellness companies
are offering employers creative strategies.*

In a complex world creating the conditions for good health is a matter of collaboration. Reducing pediatric obesity, for instance, is a challenge that depends on partnerships with children, parents, schools, health care providers, local businesses, and government, all focused on promoting healthy habits and improving quality of lifestyle. First Lady Michelle Obama has been leading this cause with her "Let's Move!" campaign accentuating healthy eating. It has drawn the kind of attention and interest needed to reverse the trend.

Similar efforts include UPMC Health Plan's "HEALTHY Armstrong" promoting "Healthy Eating Active Lifestyles Together Helping Youth" in Pennsylvania's Armstrong County School District and beyond. UPMC Health Plan partners with seven other community organizations to run the program, which has resulted in a 15% decrease in consumption of high-calorie, low-nutritional foods among participants. In Georgia, Kaiser Permanente uses "Operation Zero" to promote physical activity, educate children on healthy eating, and provide incentives for participation. Results have shown success in decreasing body fat and waist size for participants.

In the United States health insurers are emerging as leaders in developing and implementing employee wellness and health productivity initiatives. Currently, there are approximately thirty-five major private health insurance companies in the United States insuring 273 million of the 310 million Americans enrolled in a health care plan. This figure excludes Medicare providers. In addition to ensuring that their plans offer best practices that are affordable and appropriate for each of its members, many help promote health within their communities by partnering with nonprofit organizations.

BEYOND THE SILO METHOD

Since 2000, employment-based health insurance premiums have increased 87% compared to cumulative inflation of 18%.[65]

In an effort to dodge the expensive health insurance bullet, many U.S. employers with more than one thousand clients are opting to self-insure and "go at risk." These companies determine it's less expensive to pay medical claims than premiums. Part of their strategy is to purchase stop-loss insurance to protect themselves from excessive medical costs. A self-insured arrangement allows for more flexibility than benefit plans and usually involves a third-party administrator to provide access to discounted contracted networks and pay the claims that employees incur.

But how much does anyone, including employer and health insurer, know about the health of any pool of employees using the traditional silo method of care in which doctors are the only dispensers of advice and medical records are closed to protect privacy? Using this method, the health risk level of any group of employees is determined by using their anonymous aggregate claims data, pharmacy usage data, biometric screening results, and self-reported health risk assessments. The silo method simply can't reach an adequate number of employees to gather the more comprehensive information required to take actions likely to reduce risk factors and lower employer costs.

Both companies who contract with plans, and those who self-insure, know the link between health, absenteeism, presenteeism, and productivity. But they need to apply what they know. Keeping detailed records on leave management is a case in point. Employers that offer paid time off should distinguish between scheduled leave, unscheduled leave, family and medical leave, sick days, and vacation time. **The key to reducing absenteeism and improving productivity is understanding why an employee is not at work and addressing the root cause.**

A JHA absence management survey reports 55% of employee absences are blamed on disabling injuries and illnesses.[66] Good to know but not enough. A wellness program should link health-related absences to specific diagnostic codes, providing a company with quantifiable data related to the overall health and productivity of its workforce and the effect of both on its bottom line.

Employers who want to grow or strengthen their health productivity initiatives also want to know how long it'll take for their companies to reap financial benefits. While no formula exists, it takes twenty-four months to thirty-six months to make an impact on the population and start realizing a 3:1 — sometimes 6:1 — ROI. To increase participation is to increase measurable savings. To accomplish such a goal, however, requires a multi-year incremental strategy with all parties held accountable to a culture of health and an operational plan that enjoys executive support and approval.

CREATIVE PARTNERSHIPS

Benefits specialists and insurance brokers pause before investing in health productivity initiatives to ask an important question. Why should an insurer invest in expanding wellness initiatives when employees can switch carriers at renewal time and employers, in search of the lowest possible rate increase, can do likewise? The point is well taken since carrier turnover rates range from 5%-20%.

Some health plans and wellness companies, however, are offering employers creative strategies. For instance, if an employer commits to multiple years with a carrier, that carrier may agree not to raise rates the second year no matter the cost of medical services incurred. Or the carrier may offer to lock in a 2%-4 % decrease in rates over the contract period. As a condition of such an arrangement, a carrier may require a specified percentage of employees and/or dependents to participate in a health assessment, achieve biometric screening targets, and engage in some level of health coaching. With this approach, it's less likely that employer groups will change plans or partners as long as carriers are transparent in their dealings and remain competitive in pricing.

Many good independent wellness and health productivity companies also support employers, including UPMC WorkPartners, Healthways, Health Fitness, Medifit, Red Brick Health, Staywell, Mayo Clinic Health Solutions, Health Enhancement, Virgin HealthMiles, HealthMedia, and WellSteps.

WellSteps[67] offers performance guarantees up front. The company promises its employer clients that if program participation doesn't exceed 50% of all eligible participants in the first year, it will refund 20% of per employee per month

(PEPM) fees for that year. At the end of the second year, WellSteps promises that the health risk of program participants will improve by no less than 7%, or it will refund 20% of PEPM fees for that year. At the end of the third year, WellSteps guarantees significant differences in medical expenditures between participants and non-participants, up to 150% guaranteed return on investment, or it will refund 20% of PEPM fees for that year. As of this writing, WellSteps never has had to refund a customer.

Wellsteps requires, however, that the leaders of the company demonstrate personal support and have specific expectations, one being the creation of an on-site wellness committee. Champions for a wellness program must exist within a company to serve as role models for positive, sustainable behavior changes and as helpers to achieve the company's goals.

As employers evaluate wellness programs, different paradigms are emerging:

- Focusing on both medical treatment and prevention in a self-insured environment

- Hiring an independent company exclusively specializing in wellness

- Fashioning a hybrid model with health plan designers to create a healthy workplace

Remember, all wellness programs are driven by prevention, not disease. A good one accounts for many factors, including employees' claims, pharmacy costs, health assessments, biometric screenings, workers' compensation, disability, leave absences, wellness, health productivity, and employee assistance programs. Such a wellness program can even provide cross-referrals to gauge how a company's performance compares to that of others in the marketplace.

Just as importantly, these programs use the data to create changes and improvements, namely, reduce population risk levels, improve employees' health, and create savings. In addition to such customized computation and consultation, a wellness program may incorporate on-site clinics, mobile vans, and a medical home model in which primary care physicians coordinate a full continuum of care for their patients.

To maximize participation, every wellness program should be properly introduced to employees. First, the CEO of a company should either write a letter to all employees and/or otherwise publicly usher in the program. The letter should cover the rationale and benefits for the company, employees, and their families. All senior leaders need to explain the administrative process to employees.

Next, the wellness program should roll out its full array of offerings using multi-media channels, including Web portals and social media tools. A carrier with a proper communication plan and methods can target tailored messages to employer groups and in so doing engage 50% or more of an employer's total population rather than the low industry average of 25%. Even 50% falls short of the ideal participation level of at least 75%.

At the outset all employers should be clear about which services its carrier or wellness company provides free and which bear an additional cost. Generally, with an insurance carrier, all the online lifestyle and chronic condition management programs are free, as are health questionnaires, employee interest surveys, tobacco cessation programs, health fairs or events, and some health coaching. All educational printed materials, including an electronic digital newsletter and some social media tools, usually are available through a hypertext link on the website of the employer or carrier.

Marketing materials, such as fliers and posters that can be put on bulletin boards and in employee break rooms or cafeterias, also are generally free. Some may include monthly messages that coincide with the national calendar of events. February, for instance, is American Heart Month.

If a very large employer offers multiple medical carriers and health design plans from which its employees can choose, an insurance carrier may offer "wellness membership" for employees at all locations for a small monthly or yearly fee. Additional fees usually exist for biometric screenings, most campaigns, an employee assistance program, customization of integrated reports, and in-depth consultations.

THE GLOBAL MULTI-SITE CHALLENGE

Multinational Workforce Health: Building a Sustainable Global Strategy, a 2011 Towers Watson survey, shows employee health is a growing concern. Seventy-five percent of respondents expected it to be a priority for their organization in 2011 and 2012, while 87% expect the same from 2013 through 2015. Three-quarters of companies presently offer wellness programs, which are growing in popularity. **As illustrated in the following hypothetical case study, the need for a global workforce health strategy has never been greater.**

A large company that engineers and manufactures solar energy products is based in Texas but has fourteen other locations around the United States and the world. Presently, the company has twelve thousand five hundred employees and the opportunity to further expand into developed and

SUCCESS GALLERY

Kathy Newkirk

HEALTH ACHIEVEMENT:
DROPPED BLOOD GLUCOSE
LEVEL BY 92 MILLIGRAMS
PER DECILITER

EMPLOYER:
MERCY HEALTH SYSTEM,
KANSAS

JOB TITLE:
DIRECTOR OF
INSERVICE TRAINING

I was used to dieting and seeing my weight rise and fall like a yo-yo. For years I've had ten sizes of clothes in my closet and never got rid of the larger sizes because I knew I'd need them again.

Years ago, I decided that fat wasn't going to stop me from doing anything. I'd just figured, This is my life. Until July 2010 when I went to the doctor and discovered my fasting blood sugar level was a staggering 189 milligrams per deciliter (mg/dL). The meaning was clear: I'd likely get diabetes, just as many members of my family had.

I'd always known diabetes was possible but that was the first time I accepted it really could happen to me. Not liking the possibility of taking shots for the rest of my life, I contacted Sarah Patterson, a co-worker and lead dietitian at Mercy Hospital in Independence, Kansas. The first thing we did was take all processed sugars out of my diet. Sarah also set me up on a carb point system.

Now I also keep food journals and meet monthly with Judy Carpenter, a nurse, to review them. Judy's support is personal and encouraging. She's had a huge impact on my progress. I now buy more fruits and vegetables than any other food and spend most of my time shopping along the exterior walls of the grocery store where the healthier foods are.

My blood sugar is down to 97 mg/dL and I've lost sixty-six pounds. I feel good, not starved, because I'm eating the right foods, and I'm energized because I'm exercising.

My greatest motivation comes from co-workers like Sarah and others who shower me with encouragement. I've got a whole team helping me. I realize now that it's not about the size of the clothes hanging in the closet. What's more important is what's going on inside my body.

I've got to eat healthfully because my life depends on it.

underdeveloped locations in Europe, India, and Brazil. The company is continually looking for potential employees, no matter where they reside. Current employees have multi-insurance coverage that spans different carriers and varied benefits and incentives, including retiree coverage.

Enter Nick the Innovator, senior human resources director for three years and a specialist in training. Nick has been given the task of creating a more focused approach to the solar company's fragmented wellness and health productivity programs. For two years 30% of U.S. employees have had health and biometric assessments and 15% have participated minimally in programs for a variety of reasons, including the limited nature of the program offerings, lack of personalized messaging, and inconsistent incentives. Outcomes have been difficult to identify, let alone measure. Existing programs have not been offered to the global market.

As co-leaders, Nick and Jocelyn, his new wellness manager, are charged with the task of finding partners/vendors who can deliver comprehensive wellness and health population programs globally. These partners also must have the ability to offer multi-program components online, on site, telephonically, via instant chat, on demand, in digital formats, and through webinars and print modalities. In all instances, they must have the ability to increase participation levels for employees of diverse demographic backgrounds and their family members. They must offer programs that are consistent but, with a local twist and the assistance of a local manager, will appeal to employee interests, customs, traditions, and values in many countries. Additionally, the health assessments of the partners/vendors must be offered in multiple languages, adhere to America HIPAA privacy law, GINA genetic non-discrimination law, and ADA regulations. The assessments also must be adjustable for cultural differences.

As if their task wasn't formidable enough, Nick and Jocelyn also must show how employees have improved with the new programs after twenty-four months. Some measure of ROI is expected at a minimum of 3:1 to match industry standards. Ideally, they need to show significant reductions in leave absences, disability claims, and workers' compensation claims.

Nick and Jocelyn, well-traveled among the top human resources and wellness conferences, know that up to 75% of medical costs are due to modifiable lifestyle factors. They also know that two big gaps in medical care are failure to consistently take necessary medications and failure to have screenings that are age- and gender-appropriate in addition to an annual doctor's visit. Nick and Jocelyn also understand that senior management must be leaders of this effort, commit to promoting a culture of health, and provide the necessary resources and budget for the wellness programs.

The two have faced the challenges before them for some time. First, the company's health care business costs have been rising 10.5% annually while similar competitors are at a steady 8%. Second, the turnover of highly skilled employees has been too high and must be slowed or stopped.

Standard business practice for a midsize to large employer group is to collaborate with a large consulting firm like Buck, Mercer, or Willis — consultants known for their worldwide scope; research regarding programs for wellness and total health management; and specialties in benefit plan design and financial and risk issues.

Generally, a consulting firm is selected to collaborate with an employer group to formulate a set of questions, known as a Request for Proposal (RFP), which is sent to the existing vendor as well as other carriers or wellness and health productivity companies. The process proceeds as follows:

- Organizations who decide to respond to the RFP assemble an interdisciplinary team with varied specialties to write the complex, multiple answers.

- After reviewing responses, the employer chooses three to five finalists and invites each to make a one-hour presentation on why it is the best partner for the undertaking.

- A representative of the employer, along with a person from the consulting firm, conducts an on-site visit with each finalist.

- The employer awards the contract for a given number of years for a given number of dollars to one or more of the vendors.

And so another partnership begins.

AN INTERNATIONAL ALLIANCE

While we're talking about collaborating, let's think big. Envision assembling the world's best think tank experts — along with representatives of the best consultants, universities, professional organizations, government agencies, and business leaders — for the purpose of helping employer groups, carriers, and wellness companies.

This international alliance would be similar to the World Economic Forum or Global Health Workforce Alliance. It could be a place where select companies participate in the latest sharing of employee health management information and innovation.

The alliance's goal would be to help companies and individuals make better informed health decisions nationally and globally for the purpose of reducing health care costs, increasing productivity, and promoting work-life balance and morale. People from various disciplines can share what really works best and why. Such a group could be the pinnacle roundtable of wellness and health productivity for the planet. Best of all, it may set the bar to help identify and design future best practices.

BUILD YOUR BEST WELLNESS AND HEALTH MANAGEMENT PROGRAM

Answer these questions as they relate to your company:

1. Does your health insurance plan/carrier provide both basic and enhanced pricing models for wellness and health management services from which your company can choose? If so, does it also provide integrated reporting metrics?

2. Has your organization and HR department ever considered a global HR partnership? For instance, has it contemplated working with the Generali Group, one of the world's leading insurance operators, or Bupa, the world's largest expatriate health insurer with members in one hundred ninety countries?

3. Under what circumstances would you use a single wellness vendor? Under what circumstances would you use multiple partners, each with a specific expertise?

4. Can you articulate the difference between being self-insured, fully insured, and self-funded? Do you know the advantages and disadvantages of each?

5. Has your company or team been involved in the arduous process of writing and preparing documents for a Request for Proposal?

Chapter 8:

HOW INNOVATION MATTERS

In the world of health, innovation should be
a means to an end.

Innovative technology will be the key strategic driver of change that will impact global business, consumers, markets, and society, according to James Canton of the Institute for Global Futurists.[68]

But innovation means different things to different people. Some consider any new idea an innovation, while others require that it be a creative idea with a risk-taking element that leads to a new implemented product or service. Yet others contend innovation is all about change.

In the world of health, innovation should be a means to an end. For instance, how will a device or app serve a company's mission, vision, and strategic business objectives? A case in point are new technologies that help people adhere to taking medications, track compliance with a treatment plan, or improve a lifestyle risk factor, such as obesity.

Examples abound:

■ The iHealth Blood Pressure Monitoring System for the iPhone includes a blood pressure arm cuff and iPhone docking station peripheral with an app that not only monitors and tracks results but forwards them to an individual's physician.

- "My Chart," an app developed by Epic Systems and introduced by Sutter Health, can access personal electronic health records from some health companies.

- The Post-Traumatic Stress Disorder (PTSD) Coach app, available free on the iPhone and launched in April 2011 by the U.S. Department of Defense and U.S. Department of Veterans Affairs, helps military personnel and their families get immediate help or manage their symptoms.

- Signal Patterns offers psychology-based web and mobile apps that address well-being and relationships, including "Live Happy" for the iPhone, which features multiple activities and assessments and information about stress, authentic yoga, and great careers.

New Web-based trackers and tools provided by wellness vendors also can monitor daily or weekly employees' physical movements and eating habits and even keep track of how many incentive points they cumulate. Since incentive points mean premium discounts, these tools can be well used. A special pedometer with a built-in USB connection, for instance, can automatically download onto a computer the number of steps an individual has walked. Such records can prove more accurate than self-reported data.

Some health coaching can even be done in digital computer formats to make these services more scalable and less expensive to employers.

Design companies such as IDEO and Closer Look are creating design tools to improve people's engagement levels and entice them to view other quality content and services.

Designers are borrowing a page from the gaming industry and building gamification into their devices. They've discovered the importance of creating a journey, or story, to lead an employee from one incremental small step to another in an overall march toward changing unhealthy behaviors and sustaining healthy ones.

In his 2010 book, *Innovate the Future: A Radical New Approach to IT Innovation*, David Croslin[69] explains how a customer perceives and uses a product and determines whether it's innovative or competitive with existing products. Croslin measures a product's "transformative value" and contends an individual evaluates a product in terms of how it will change his life or business. No matter how many features are wrapped into a product, according to Croslin, people see it as transformational in three ways: Will the product save time? Will the product save or make money? Will the product simplify life? Highly successful innovative products such as the iPhone, Blackberry, Kindle Fire, or iPad easily pass his tests of transformation.

How does a company start to become innovative in wellness? Just as with a culture of health, a culture of innovation starts at the top of the corporate ladder. In his 2010 book *Blogging Innovation*,[70] Kamal Hassan, head of Innovation 360 Institute, describes three styles of company innovation:

1. **Idea marketplace innovation.** These companies place a high value on employee idea generation. Employees are recruited not only for their skills, but also creativity and passion. This open-minded atmosphere is reflected in companies such as Google and IBM.

2. **Visionary leader innovation.** These companies rely on the brilliance and charisma of a senior executive. It's difficult to think of Apple without thinking of Steve Jobs. Or to think of the Virgin Group without bringing to mind Sir Richard Branson, who also has an outstanding wellness company, Virgin HealthMiles. Everyone at such companies works to fulfill the leader's ideas through creative problem solving.

3. **Systematic innovation.** More traditional companies such as GE, Nokia, and Procter & Gamble still solicit and enhance employee contributions and develop ideas systematically using corporate roadmaps and project management measures.

All three styles share common themes. They challenge tradition; encourage new thinking; raise the bar for trust, communication and teamwork; and acknowledge the differences between ideas and incremental and disruptive innovation.

In *Stoking Your Innovation Bonfire*,[71] Braden Kelley writes innovation is not just about a project. Projects start and stop, but innovation doesn't. **Innovation is about adapting to changes in the marketplace.** It's about a company finding new solutions that customers value above every existing alternative, including that company's current products and services.

As a process innovation involves both divergent thinking (expanding a list of possibilities) and convergent thinking (reducing a list of possibilities). For instance, a wellness committee that applies divergent thinking may say, "Let's investigate the tools we want to use to measure outcomes for a stress and well-being campaign in the workplace — webinars, media tools, and other IT resources." Meanwhile, other wellness

SUCCESS GALLERY

Lucy Freixas

HEALTH ACHIEVEMENT:
DECREASED BLOOD PRESSURE
AS WELL AS A IC AND CHOLES-
TEROL LEVELS

EMPLOYER:
BAPTIST HEALTH SOUTH FLORIDA

JOB TITLE:
CORPORATE CONTRACT
COMPLIANCE SUPERVISOR

The My Unlimited Potential program has impacted my life in more positive ways than I could have ever imagined. I've always desired to reach my health goals but never knew how to start or what to do. The program, however, provided all the necessary medical tools, such as glucose and blood pressure monitors, as well as support and motivation in the form of a dietitian and personal training classes.

When I started the program I was on blood pressure medication that my doctor has had to decrease with the ultimate goal of weaning me off it. My A1C levels also decreased from 7.0% to 6.3%. My cholesterol levels decreased as well.

Additionally, I have lost ten pounds to date and decreased several dress sizes. I sleep and feel well and my energy level is magnificent.

I am very grateful to work for a company such as Baptist Health South Florida that provides the opportunity to learn the value and importance of good diet and exercise. The program transformed my outlook toward health and wellness, and I plan on continuing my new healthy lifestyle.

committee members who apply convergent thinking may say, "Let's focus on a few outcome measures pertaining specifically to pre- and post-assessments on resiliency." Both approaches help clarify the benefits and pitfalls of any innovation.

Determining which types of innovation serve a particular company requires staying open to ideas from everyone, especially wellness committee members who also can apply lateral thinking, that is, new out-of-the-box creative solutions that are inexpensive.

CONNECTING WITH INSPIRATION

Health care specialists at any company can find support for their own projects and ideas if they look in the right places.

The Agency for Healthcare Research and Quality,[72] sponsored by the U.S. Department of Health and Human Services, is an excellent source to help companies address innovation. Its website discusses three factors to be considered when making decisions regarding innovation:

- Organizational priorities
- Likely impact of innovative solutions
- Capacity to innovate

These three sets of considerations may appear to be sequential but also must be considered in parallel. Most important is finding low-hanging fruit that will give a company the most bang for its buck. These fruits present themselves as doable, realistic steps that can be taken right away.

The Agency for Healthcare Research and Quality has produced *Connecting Those at Risk to Care: A Guide to Building a Community Hub*, an invaluable guide to anyone in the health care industry. Its website also has a "Learn and Network" section featuring experts and practitioners who are encouraged to share innovative ideas that could work within circumstantial parameters set by visitors to the site.

Sometimes inspiration can come inside the morning newspaper. In September 2008, for instance, Stephanie Stron wrote in *The New York Times*[73] about the Broad Institute of MIT and Harvard, which works to discover genetic links to major diseases and determines the molecular causes of disease. While it's true that discoveries could lead to new ways to diagnose and prevent illnesses, the way the institute works is in itself sheer innovation.

Both universities and their research staffs are fiercely competitive. Yet the institute links multi-disciplinary scientists to work in collaborative partnerships with common goals, even though in some cases the scientists are in different physical locations throughout the world. Dr. Eric Lander, who heads the institute, was a principal leader of the Human Genome Project.

Innovation at work

Leading universities, health centers, and carriers are innovating wellness initiatives all over the nation. Here's a glimpse at some key efforts:

The University of Pittsburgh Medical Center (UPMC), a $9 billion global health enterprise in Pittsburgh, Pennsylvania, prides itself on being a life-changing medical resources organization. With almost fifty-five thousand employees, it is transforming health care by integrating twenty-two hospitals, four hundred doctors' offices, outpatient sites, long-term care facilities, a health insurance service division, and international and commercial services.

UPMC also is redefining health care by using innovative science, technology, and medicine to invent new models of accountable, cost-efficient, and patient-centered care. UPMC Presbyterian Hospital, for example, is participating in a focused-readmission pilot tracking congestive heart failure. For more than a year, the care team has tested varied interventions such as enhanced care coordination, interactive patient educational modules, and continuum of care after discharge. Preliminary results show a reduction in readmission rate in congestive heart failure from 27% to 15% and a decrease in the average length of stay from 14.3 to 10.2 days.

UPMC's innovative MyHealth suite of wellness programs and services maintains and improves the health and productivity of its thirty-four thousand employees even as it reduces their risk factors and UPMC's health cost trend. Since MyHealth's 2004 launch, UPMC senior leadership has been fully supportive and more than ninety percent of employees have participated every year.

Launched in 2009, the "Take a Healthy Step" incentive platform offers employees personalized suggestions for health improvement measures. An impressive 114,807 healthy steps were taken by employees at twenty-six business locations in 2011 alone.

Between 2008 and 2010, results across UPMC included a 39.9% to 46.2% increase in employees meeting recommended guidelines for physical activity; a 18.1% to 12.3% decrease in smoking prevalence; and an 87.1% to 84.4% decrease in employees at nutritional risk.

In 2011, while many employers experienced high single-digit to double-digit increases in employee medical and pharmaceutical costs, UPMC enjoyed a cost trend of just about one percent. The same year the percentage of UPMC employees at the very lowest health risk level increased from 76.8% to 76.9%. Simultaneously, the percentage with the highest risk level shrunk from 4.3% to 3.9%.

Meanwhile, Andrew Watson, MD, vice president of the international commercial division for the UPMC System, is working on telemedicine, which he believes is the natural evolution of health care in the world of the cloud. Dr. Watson visualizes a central command station where nurses, allied health professionals, health coaches, and others could provide quality treatment virtually anywhere. Under his leadership, the UPMC System is working with Alcatel-Lucent to build one of the world's first platforms to leverage technology, staff, administrative processes, scheduling, and telemedicine protocols. He anticipates such an operation to be ready for the fourth quarter of 2012.

UPMC also uses advanced information technology to assure quality and safety in patient care and to streamline business practices. For instance, UPMC hosts the Peter M. Winter Institute for Simulation, Education, and Research (WISER) where clinicians train in new surgical techniques on computerized mannequins as well as in realistic mock scenarios, including bioterrorism attacks and Medevac helicopters. Another innovation is e-Record, UPMC's electronic health record system.

A botanist and pioneer in the field of integrative medicine, Andrew Weil, MD, has devoted his life to developing, teaching, and practicing an innovative natural healing approach to health and wellness. Embraced by millions worldwide, his philosophy draws on both alternative and mainstream medicine and emphasizes mind, body, and spiritual balance. Dr. Weil, whose most recent book is *Spontaneous Happiness*, also is founder and director of the **Arizona Center for Integrative Medicine** at the University of Arizona Health Sciences in Tucson. He also:

- Developed the first comprehensive academic curriculum in integrative medicine

- Created the first combined residency in family medicine and integrative medicine in the United States

- Co-founded the Consortium of Academic Health Centers for Integrative Medicine

The **Princeton Longevity Center**[74] in Princeton, New Jersey, is another organization that contributes to enhanced life. Noting cardiovascular disease is the leading cause of death in America, the longevity center cites the fact that sudden death is the first symptom for one of every three people who develop coronary disease. Generally, though, it takes twenty or more years for plaque to build up in arteries to the point a person is at high enough risk for a heart attack or stroke. Finding plaque early means easier, more effective treatment.

According to the center's physicians, 68% of heart attacks occur when arteries are less than 50% narrowed; however, traditional stress tests do not reveal abnormalities until an artery is at least 70% narrowed. Studies also have shown that 70% of heart attacks occur in people with normal cholesterol levels.

Until recently, doctors couldn't tell which person with high cholesterol might have coronary disease requiring medication and which had clear arteries with very little risk. But cardiac CT scans changed that reality. Now doctors can painlessly and non-invasively look directly at the arteries with a 64-slice CT coronary angiography to see how much plaque is present. With the resulting Coronary Calcium Score, which measures

DANCING WITHOUT SHOES IN DR. STUDENSKI'S RESEARCH LAB

One floor of Dr. Stephanie Studenski's lab, located in the UPMC Kaufmann Medical Building near the University of Pittsburgh, is dedicated to a wide range of exercise and physical activity programs, including video games, DVDs with music and dance, and 32"x32" Dance Dance Revolution non-slip sensor pads.

The technology is connected so when music starts playing, a person ready to exercise can follow a television monitor that features four to eight fully functioning directional arrows which point up, down, right, and left. The objective is to coordinate one's feet to the pattern of arrows on the screen, which move at varying fast speeds, and keep the rhythm going to the various songs selected. The songs have easy, intermediate, hard, and extreme scoring mechanisms.

Dr. Studenski's interest in this work started eight years ago when she discovered that video dance helped her meet her personal health goals, including losing fifty pounds. The key to her success, she thought, was the recreational, interesting nature of the exercise, which helped her view it as fun rather than duty.

Wondering if such games could be useful to others, she conducted several research projects with postmenopausal women and other healthy older adults. Results supported that video dancing helped people to exercise and improve overall physical and brain health, and aided in preventing falls.

After trying out the dances for fun at her lab, I decided to purchase equipment. Dr. Studenski came to my home to set it up. I invited several other women from our health plan and Dr. Studenski explained to all of us how her method works. Between the individual lessons, we enjoyed red wine, cheese, and lots of laughter. When any of us were able to follow one or two patterns correctly, we all cheered.

Always having been athletic, I thought the routines would be easy and I'd be well on my way to earning an A or B score rather easily. But at first I earned a lot of Ds and even an F, but I kept practicing. In four weeks I was earning consistent As, which meant I'd conquered and passed that skill level. To continue challenging myself, I'd have to graduate to more difficult songs with more intricate movement patterns. I was so proud of my accomplishments that I had to photograph the TV monitor which showed my A scores so I could send a picture with the results to my two sisters.

the amount of calcium deposits in the walls of the arteries, doctors can gauge a person's heart attack risk as quickly as a blood pressure cuff can measure hypertension. The higher the calcium score, the greater the likelihood of a potential heart attack or future coronary event.

Humana Inc.,[75] one of the largest health companies in the country, covers almost 12 million people. For many years it has operated its Humana Innovation Center, an internal think tank that talks to consumers and comes up with better, creative ways to engage people and help them stay or get healthier. Remember, informed consumers can make better health care decisions and healthier choices.

The company website has an avatar called "Meet Diabatron" who monitors twitter daily and picks up the top twenty people talking about a particular health condition, such as diabetes, as well as related topics. His role is making it easy for people with diabetes, and those who care for them, to connect with others going through the same challenges. Participants share their knowledge, information, support, and encouragement with each other.

Humana also is conducting interesting campaigns with its Freewheelin' bike sharing program in which a person gets to borrow a bike and return it later. Each bike measures the rider's biometrics, including pulse and weight, and calculates his effort while pedaling. To promote exercise among various age populations, and especially people over fifty, the Humana Innovation Center also is experimenting with video games using Wii and Dance Dance Revolution Dance Pads. The goals: improving movement, balance, concentration, and memory. Humana's primary researcher on the effects of dancing on health is Stephanie Studenski, MD, a leading gerontologist and research professor and physician from the University of Pittsburgh.

Yet another innovation is the stand-alone upscale retail store known as **Max-Wellness,**[76] started by Michael Feuer, past owner of OfficeMax stores which he sold for $1.5 billion after an initial investment of twenty thousand dollars. Feuer spent time visiting fitness centers as well as drug, vitamin, and footwear stores and now has six, one-stop wellness shopping stores in Ohio and Florida and plans for nationwide expansion. Each store is supplied with more than seven thousand health-related products and offers health screenings, fairs, and product discounts.

Products also can be purchased via catalogs and online at www. max-wellness.com. One example of an innovative wellness product is Dakim BrainFitness, clinically tested software for people over sixty. In twenty minutes a day the software delivers challenging graphic games, tests, and puzzles that comprise a comprehensive brain fitness workout to keep the mind sharp and help stave off memory loss and cognitive decline. Another product is a therapeutic cervical pillow with fillable water that provides comfort and support to the head and neck and reduces neck pain even as it improves quality of sleep.

Max-Wellness also is working on other initiatives. Mini-Max, a smaller version of a store, is now available adjacent to gift shops in select hospitals. Mini-Max provides patients with products they need to help their recovery at home. Feuer also innovated Wellness-in-a-Box, computerized vending machines containing health items appropriate to their locations. They are to appear in a variety of venues, including urgent care centers, assisted living facilities, airports, and fitness centers.

Feuer calls his employees "wellness associates" and started his own "wellness academy" sales training program.

SUCCESS GALLERY

Michael Schall

HEALTH ACHIEVEMENT: DROPPED BLOOD GLUCOSE LEVEL BY
300 MILLIGRAMS PER DECILITER
EMPLOYER: UPMC
JOB TITLE: MEDICAL ASSISTANCE ELIGIBILITY SPECIALIST

My diabetes diagnosis took me by surprise. A lab test confirmed my blood sugar level was more than 400 milligrams per deciliter (mg/dL) and my doctor prescribed medication. I, however, decided it was time for a lifestyle change, too.

In my job as a medical assistance eligibility specialist, I interact with younger people who reside in UPMC skilled nursing facilities, several because of complications due to diabetes.

I have two sons, and I want to be around for them. So I joined the UPMC Health Plan Weigh to Wellness™ program and worked weekly by phone with health coach Janine Jones to lose weight and get my blood sugar under control.

In a matter of two weeks, my blood sugar level went from 400 to 150 mg/dL. Within two more months it was consistently under 100 mg/dL. Eventually, it averaged well below 100 mg/dL, and I asked my physician if the medication could be discontinued. My physician was amazed at the turnaround and said he wished other patients would take their conditions as seriously.

Janine got me so skinny that in six months I lost more than thirty-five pounds. She taught me how to eat healthfully without being hungry. I'm never hungry. If I really want something, like Italian bread or a fried food, I'll have it occasionally. But I limit myself and watch portions. I also monitor my intake of carbohydrates.

Getting my health back was an important result of my work with Janine, but it wasn't the only result. My pants size went from a thirty-eight to a thirty-two.

Today I'm in better physical shape than Evan, my eighteen-year-old son who exercises and plays deck hockey regularly. Due to my daily regimen of weight training morning and evening, I have abs again. I haven't seen my abs in decades!

I also take ten thousand steps a day, including a daily two-mile walk, and am now at the right weight for motorcycle racing.

I'm very happy with the changes I've made and thankful that UPMC Health Plan was there for me.

Build Your Best Wellness and Health Management Program

Answer these questions as they relate to your company:

1. Can you articulate a type of innovative product, service, or project presently in your organization?

2. Has your organization teamed up and partnered with a nonprofit organization for a bigger and better community good?

3. Can you think of a wellness company, agency, or center whose ideas and programs can benefit your organization?

4. If your supervisor assigned you to research health and wellness gaps within your organization, would you feel comfortable taking on this task?

5. Give an example of how an innovative product has transformed consumers' lives and enhanced the brand, customer loyalty, and profits of the manufacturer.

Chapter 9:

THE HEALING POWER OF SOCIAL MEDIA

More than one thousand one hundred eighty-eight U.S. hospitals use social media.

People who want to improve their behaviors and health enjoy turning to social media tools that include the latest science from reliable sources such as WebMD, Mayo Clinic, Johns Hopkins Medicine, Harvard Medical School, and the Centers for Disease Control and Prevention. Although the general public cannot control the conversation at such sites, they still like to contribute with questions and answers, instant chats, or text messaging.

According to an October 2011 report by iHealth Beat, the Consumer Electronics Association found that 36% of consumers are interested in using mobile health tools to communicate with their health care providers. In addition, 33% of survey respondents said they're interested in managing their health records online while 32% said they'd like to use telehealth tools for physician visits.

Such tools can be effective in maintaining participation in online health programs, according to a University of Michigan Medical School study.[77] Researchers found adding an interactive social media site to an Internet-based walking program significantly lowered the number of participants who dropped out. The study showed 79% of participants who used an online forum for group motivation remained in the sixteen-week program, while only 65% of those who used the website without the social media components finished. These findings also indicate that adding social media tools to an online program can reduce costs associated with traditional interventions, such as on-site meetings.

It follows that a company-customized campaign created for a specific employee population can tally even greater success rates. Social media provides willing employees an alternate universe of support. In the real world, people are helped by peer influence. In the virtual world, those messages of support are reinforced with YouTube, video clips, blogs, user forums, Twitter, and Facebook.

Social media tools engage consumers in meaningful two-way conversations that enable them to influence product improvement and customer service efforts. But those conversations also are happening between and among consumers. **Here's an important reality check: Consumers are now the chief influencers of other consumers.** How might such knowledge be put to use for the benefit of health care providers and consumers? Consider that women make 85% of household health decisions, including choice of doctors and hospital loyalty, a statistic well known to hospital executives. It behooves any hospital marketing department, then, to feature a podcast and blog about women's health and family issues on its website.

Anyone who wants to help a company select and use the best social media tools for its wellness and health management initiatives first must understand their scope and power. There are more than two billion Web users, according to www.InternetWorldStats.com.[78] Asia has more than 825 million users. The United States has approximately 267 million users, almost 78% of its population. Use is highest among those eighteen to twenty-nine years old.

Among those who are fifty to sixty-five years old, however, Web use has increased from 25% to 47% in one year's time, according to an August 2010 Pew research study.[79] Baby boomers are flocking to the social networks. In all, 78% of them maintain a Facebook profile. Currently, 75% of American adults and 95% of teenagers have access to the Internet. Broadband is in two-thirds of American homes. In all, 80% of Americans have cell phones and six out of ten use them as their only phone.[80]

Even as Web 4.0 technologies enter the marketplace, many people have integrated Web 3.0 technologies into their daily lives and use integrated and personalized platforms to get coupons, discounts and tags, make store purchases, buy music and books, gather health information, schedule doctor appointments, receive reminders, and use Gmail, email, and Skype.

AN INTERDISCIPLINARY EFFORT

Like any strategy, it's important to begin a social media campaign by identifying objectives. Before making any financial or human capital investment, ask:

- What are its objectives?
- Who is the targeted audience?
- What is the budget?
- What is efficient to monitor and maintain?

- Who will be accountable for monitoring and measuring results?

- What are local competitors in health care doing?

In many organizations these functions cross disciplinary lines and include the marketing and communications and information technology departments as well as clinical staff, who usually are the content experts. In *Engage*, Brian Solis,[81] a respected thought leader in new media, writes that social media is less about technology and more about sociology, anthropology, and the environment. He reports we can't measure what we don't recognize as valuable and clarifies four elements for measuring the influence of a social media campaign:

1. **Exposure** To what degree have we created exposure to content and message?

2. **Engagement** Who is interacting with the content? When and how are they doing so?

3. **Influence** To what degree has exposure to and engagement with the content influenced perceptions and attitudes?

4. **Action** As a result of the effort, what actions, if any, have transpired?

Other potential measurement metrics include number of emails received, percentage of increase in visitor traffic, clicks from Facebook pages to portals, number of click-throughs to survey questions, and number of re-tweets and blog comments.

But there are many important factors to consider when writing a policy for social media campaigns that must be taken seriously since they carry some inherent risks for providers, insurers, and consumers. There are technical issues of encryption, auto-reply, and other features for consumer safety in emergency situations. There are clinical issues of subject content limitations, and legal issues, including patient acknowledgment of disclaimer policies and retention of content ownership.

When mounting such a campaign, a wellness committee also must ensure the privacy and protection of everyone who participates. Other best practices include addressing head-on any negative discussions that begin, and correcting factual errors that surface without being critical or mentioning names.

At the outset of any social media campaign planning, consulting in-house counsel for advice is key. There are other sources of help, too, such as the federal government at http://www.howto.gov/social-media and the Social Media Business Council, http://www.socialmedia.org , where companies share and learn from each other's social media experiences. Those who prefer an already well-established tool kit for social media can look into buying one from an experienced specialized company such as Benz Communications[82] founded by Jennifer Benz, its chief strategist.

SOCIAL MEDIA IN ACTION

It's helpful to see how some health companies are using social media tools to help employees change behavior. Recently, they are using such tools to:

- Attract new patients and their families

- Communicate information using a more personalized, targeted methodology

- Increase awareness about specialty providers, services, and programs

- Call people to action to engage them and keep them engaged

Currently, more than one thousand one hundred eight-eight U.S. hospitals use social media; one thousand seventy-four have Facebook pages, and seven hundred fifty have Twitter accounts. In all, 93% of electronically engaged patients say the Internet has made it possible to obtain medical data they want.[83] Here are ways social media are being put to good use:

- **Henry Ford Hospital** in Detroit, Michigan, was the first hospital to tweet a live surgery. This hospital also maintains multiple Facebook pages, blogs, and YouTube channels for its diverse audiences.

- **Scott & White Hospital** in Fort Hood, Texas, used social media tools for crisis management in November 2009 when an Army psychiatrist opened fire at Fort Hood, killing twelve people and wounding thirty-one others. Before the first shooting victim arrived in the emergency room, the hospital posted an update to its Twitter account: Refer to our homepage http://www.sw.org for statements re: Ft Hood incidents #fthood #forthood. It was followed by re-tweets from the American Red Cross, led to dialogues with local reporters, and provided other resources for visitors.

- In 2010 the **Mayo Clinic Center for Social Media,**

http://socialmedia.mayoclinic.org , was launched to help bring the voices of patients, patient advocates, and caregivers into clinical conversations. It provides information, connects patients with doctors, and inspires healthy choices throughout its medical network.

- **Aetna** encourages health through social gaming by collaborating with Mindbloom, a company that has created an online game designed to promote a healthy and balanced life with meaning. Its motto is, "It's like that farm game, only way more meaningful." Together, Aetna and Mindbloom are blending gaming, technology, art, and behavioral psychology to engage people on their mobile phones with a virtual reward system that helps them achieve their personal wellness goals. Do visit http://www.mindbloom.com . (For more about the benefits of gaming in general, do visit Jane McGonigal, PhD, at http://www.avantgame.com .)

- Innovation-friendly **Humana**, whose initiatives were partially covered in Chapter 8, also sends health alerts to certain health plan members that include reminders about flu shots, mammograms, or colon exams. These alerts help satisfy the Healthcare Effectiveness Data and Information Set (HEDIS) requirements of the National Quality Forum. They are dispatched through MyHumana Mobile iPhone and Android apps for their members. At the 2011 Online Media, Marketing and Advertising Global Conference, these apps won in the medical category at the first-ever Appy Awards.

- The **Cigna** Mobile website, http://www.cigna.com/mobile , permits members to use mobile devices in Spanish and English to locate network providers, facilities, and pharmacies. Members also can review covered drugs, search for generic equivalents, and compare prices.

■ **Blue Cross and Blue Shield of North Carolina** launched HealthNAV, its own apps and mobile website, with iPhone, iPad, and iPod. They help users find the closest urgent care center.[84]

■ The **Office on Smoking and Health** in the **Centers for Disease Control and Prevention** created its own Facebook fan page, CDC Tobacco Free, enabling it to reach individuals and organizations with reliable, up-to-date information on tobacco-related topics. The Facebook page also allows the office to partner with organizations to share resources and services at the national, state, and local levels. Various materials in different media tool formats can be viewed, downloaded, and shared.

■ **Shape Up**, http://www.shapeup.com , a wellness company with a solid social network platform that services one hundred fifty corporate employers, gets on average 30%-50% employee participation without incentives and 60%-90% participation with incentives.

■ **UPMC Health Plan** members can use mobile devices to access a personal health record, review claims data, locate network providers and pharmacies, and access a virtual identification card. They also can receive reminders on preventive care.

■ **CDPHP**'s Find-A-Doc Mobile allows the plan's members to review network providers and driving directions.

■ **Health Net** offers Health Net Mobile, permitting

its members to access their identification card and eligibility information, which can be photocopied at doctors' offices.

■ **Highmark, Inc.** launched the Health@Hand phone app in 2010. In addition to getting information about providers and pharmacies, its members can use the app to search for information about illnesses, symptoms, and medical conditions.

E-POWER TO THE PATIENT

A report by Computer Sciences Corporation[85] looks ahead at new technologies that will control costs even as they improve health and self-monitoring and increase earlier detection of diseases. The findings assure us that use of social media to promote health is a trend that will grow. Here are some key trends identified in the report:

■ Patients will be more empowered regarding their care management on a daily basis with monitoring devices that allow the rapid exchange of vital medical data between patient and provider.

■ Smartphones will function as mini computers to aid patients and alert doctors to changes in patients' conditions.

■ In the next five years an estimated 1.4 billion people will use smartphones worldwide, and more than one of three people who do so will use a health-related app.

■ Presently, mobile apps help people lose weight and stay healthy. Another category of apps will provide a reference guide to drugs that can be used to check drug interactions and identify pills.

- Technological robots will assist patients with health coaching and lifestyle changes.

The worlds of health and technology now seem forever married, and the beauty for a wellness program is that tools and media channels can be mixed and matched to best suit the needs of any employee population, subpopulation, or individual. The goal always is to provide rich, quality content twenty-four/seven and strive to keep people engaged in ongoing activities and interventions.

BUILD YOUR BEST WELLNESS AND
HEALTH MANAGEMENT PROGRAM

Answer these questions as they relate to your company:

1. Has your company leveraged social media tools to engage more members and their families in wellness initiatives? If so, who is responsible for monitoring and tracking outcomes beyond the number of website hits?

2. Does your company have an interdisciplinary team charged with developing and promoting strategies to measure outcomes of social media campaigns?

3. Do you know what percentage of your company's employees and members are actively using the websites and/or social media tools available to them to help them improve their lifestyles and manage chronic conditions?

4. Has your company offered staff training as to what social media tools exist and how to use them properly?

5. Do your employees enjoy the delivery of health coaching offered online, on site, by phone, or through instant chat? If yes, in the immediate future will your company be willing to explore computer-generated health coaching and technological health coaching robots?

Chapter 10:

AIMING FOR EXCELLENCE

Awards exist for companies of all sizes and at all developmental phases of workplace programs — introducing, delivering, expanding, and evaluating.

Constant evaluation is a hallmark of a good wellness and health management program that yields health improvement and financial dividends.

Some companies show their commitment to quality by voluntarily seeking accreditation from organizations with solid reputations, including the National Committee for Quality Assurance (NCQA)[86] and Utilization Review Accreditation Commission (URAC).[87] Periodically, these companies undergo a vigorous review that evaluates their programs.

As of 2009, the NCQA offers *Standards and Guidelines for Accreditation in Wellness and Health Promotion*, a publication, and Survey Tools, technical specifications to help companies ready themselves for submitting materials to NCQA.

In November 2008, URAC launched standards and measures specific to health plans and wellness organizations. For more information, check the URAC Policy Maker Resource Center at http://www.urac.org/policyMakers/resources .

AN ARRAY OF AWARDS

Besides accreditation, awards validate the commitment and hard work people put into total health management programs. Awards exist for companies of all sizes and at all developmental phases of workplace programs — introducing, delivering, expanding, and evaluating.

Companies of all sizes are eligible to enter the American Heart Association's[88] **Start! Fit-friendly Companies Award** that calls for excellence in creating a culture that promotes physical activity and healthy eating. The application is easy to complete online and offers awards at both the gold and platinum levels. The association provides Stay Fit, a free tool kit containing everything a company needs to immediately start a physical activity campaign.

The American College of Occupational and Environmental Medicine[89] (ACOEM) offers an award that honors organizations in the United States with exemplary worker health, safety, and environmental management programs. The college has a thorough **Corporate Health Achievement Award** checklist and scoring system that focuses on four key categories: leadership and management, healthy workers, environment, and the organization. There's a charge for the application and a follow-up with site reviewers. The most current winner is Baptist Health South Florida.

The American Psychological Association[90] offers a **Psychologically Healthy Workplace Award** that recognizes organizations for their efforts in fostering employee health and well-being while enhancing organizational performance. eXude Benefits Group in Philadelphia, Pennsylvania, is a perfect example of a small company that has won this award. It services more than two hundred fifty employer groups twenty-four/seven and is known for its outstanding customer service. For more information, do visit www.phwa.org .

"I want my thirty-three employees to have fun and to know this is a great place to work where people are recognized, appreciated, and can grow with the company as much as they like," said Marcos Lopez, founder and CEO. "My philosophy is that we are all adults who treat each other with respect, so I let them have control over their own schedules." Most of his employees are women in their early thirties who have flexible work schedules and work in teams. If an employee needs to attend a special event, plan a wedding, or extend a maternity leave, she can get the time off, but only if the team can cover the workload.

Lopez designed a gym, weight room, and showers, and permits employees to use the facilities before, during, or after work. He added a full kitchen for employees who choose to bring food from home, or just relax. eXude also offers educational on-site speakers as well as informal yoga classes and running events. Employees are paid for time they volunteer with community charities, and the company donates one hundred thousand dollars annually to community nonprofits. For these reasons eXude has won the American Psychological Association state award in 2010 and national award in 2011, even as it consistently has been rated one of the Best Places to Work in PA. eXude is one of the fastest growing companies in Inc. 500 and its overall revenue growth continues to climb.

Relevant especially for hospitals is the **HealthLeaders Media Award.**[91] Its emphasis is on recognizing the most effective leadership teams that improve member health and decrease costs. Categories include large hospitals and health systems; community and midsize hospitals; small health plans; and medical group practices.

With regard to Employee Assistance Programs, the main organization is the **Employee Assistance Society of North America (EASNA),**[92] which annually bestows two corporate awards for excellence, one to a Canadian company and one to an American company. For 2011 the American winner was Home Depot, whose EAP vendor is ValueOptions. Nominations are reviewed by a panel of judges seeking to identify companies that have worked in partnership with EAP providers to design and integrate a program that enhances employees' well-being. The program also is judged in terms of how it enables a company to work toward a healthy, productive workforce. Check out the organization's electronic one-page checklist at http://www.easna.org .

Wellness Council of America (WELCOA)[93] bestows **Well Workplace Awards** in Bronze, Silver, Gold and Platinum categories to companies of all sizes. The bronze award recognizes companies laying the foundation for building a results-oriented program by incorporating the Seven Benchmark Model:

1. Obtaining CEO and senior leadership support

2. Forming a wellness team or committee that is up and running

3. Collecting data

4. Creating an operational plan

5. Offering interventions

7. Showing cultural significance

7. Preparing to measure outcomes

The silver award also requires evidence of a supportive environment to modify health risks and improve health. The gold award, for companies that have successfully built comprehensive wellness initiatives, requires statistical evidence that the program works. Lastly, the platinum award, only given to companies that already have won the gold, recognizes innovations effective for health and the bottom line.

To date, more than one thousand companies throughout the United States have met these criteria and been placed on the list that represents some of America's healthiest organizations. For more details, do visit http://www.wellworkplaceawards.org . The WELCOA award does require membership and an annual fee of $365.

The **Health Enhancement Research Organization** (HERO), a national leader in the creation of employee health management, honors companies at its annual conference.

The **C. Everett Koop National Health Award**[94] is for midsize and large companies that can show their programs have caused chronic lifestyle changes among employees that have rippled into the community. To qualify, a program must exist a minimum of two years and be in sync with the goals and objectives of the federal Healthy People 2010 and Healthy People 2020 initiatives. Savings may include both direct and indirect costs related to leave absence management, workers' compensation, and medical bills. Companies that have won in recent years include Lincoln Industries, L.L.Bean, Alliance Data, Nationwide Mutual Insurance Company, Medical Mutual of Ohio, Pfizer, and Volvo.

LESSONS FROM L.L.BEAN

L.L.Bean, Inc., a leading multi-channel merchant of quality outdoor gear and apparel with more than five thousand employees, has won the distinguished C. Everett Koop National Health Award. A leader in employee wellness, the company also has received star status with OSHA – Voluntary Protection Programs in several of its facilities for achieving high safety levels.

Susan Tufts manages Healthy Lifestyles, L.L.Bean's comprehensive Employee Wellness Program, which has been in place since 1982. The program, which comprises health risk assessments and benefits, offers free on-site preventive screenings on company time. More than 85% of employees have participated in the program, which requires three steps for lower premium rates:

1. Complete a Health Risk Assessment annually using WebMD

2. Participate in a biometric screening every other year

3. Complete a minimum of one call with a health coach, regardless of risk level. Participants with moderate and high risks are eligible to receive multiple calls with a coach but are only required to have the first call.

L.L.Bean has an on-site health clinic offering the services of a physician, physician's assistant, physical therapist, and registered nurses. It also has launched many successful, targeted health initiatives. For instance, the company went smoke free in its buildings in 1993, a move that resulted in smoking levels dropping from 20% in 1993 to 15% in 1995. In

2005 the company took the initiative a step further and went tobacco free on its grounds. Over the next four years, smoking rates dropped from 12% to 7%.

When obesity was found to be at 64% at one of the company's contact centers, L.L.Bean developed a comprehensive year-long weight management program that focused on exercise, nutrition, and mental health. Employees who wished to participate were required to apply for the program. All twenty-four applicants who met the criteria were accepted. Employees were paid to exercise in group sessions with an exercise instructor three times per week for the first six months, twice a week for the next three months, and once a week for the last three months. As the class progressed and the number of paid classes decreased, the expectation was that participants would increase the amount of exercise they did on unpaid time. In addition, they attended nutrition classes every other week, completed daily dietary logs, and attended mental health classes monthly, all on paid company time.

L.L.Bean's ROI shows impressive results. Using the formula of total program costs to total savings, the company achieved a benefit cost ratio of 1.7:1 for 2007, 2.3:1 for 2008, and 5.3:1 for 2009. These figures include medical costs only and don't tally added savings in absenteeism and presenteeism.

Another award offered for companies of all sizes is the **Corporate Health and Productivity Management Awards** of the Institute for Health and Productivity Management (IHPM).[95] Criteria focus on corporate commitment and program innovation as well as health and economic outcomes. For purposes of these awards, small companies are those with fewer than five hundred employees, while midsize companies have five hundred to five thousand employees, and large companies, more than five thousand. Do explore further at http://www.ihpm.org/awards .

Large companies may want to pursue awards given by the **National Business Group on Health (NBGH)**,[96] which also has various levels. In all, sixty-six large employers, including thirteen first-time winners, were presented with the 2010 Best Employers for Healthy Lifestyles Awards. The goal of the program is to encourage all employers to take action. Winners are honored in three categories: platinum for established workplace well-being programs with documented successful outcomes; gold for the creation of cultural and environmental changes that support long-term behavioral changes; and silver for employers who have started programs or services to promote a healthier lifestyle.

To achieve the platinum award, mature companies must complete the Wellness Impact Scorecard (WISCORE) offered online. Here are examples of platinum-level award-winning programs in 2010:

- **Baptist Health South Florida** created its Wellness Advantage in 2001. The program offers free on-site employee health clinics, an innovative weight-loss portfolio, and an award-winning video library focusing on prevention and safety.

- **Intel Corporation**'s Health for Life offers assessments, fitness programs, seminars, flu prevention services, on-site clinics, and personalized wellness coaching. All are offered in the United States and at international sites.

- **Mayo Clinic** offers on-site resources and programs, including healthy options through the employee food service, free health screenings, a nicotine dependence center, and collaboration with community organizations. Also offered are a healthy living center where employees go for all lifestyle programs, health coaching, educational materials, and condition trackers. Reward points are used as incentives.

- **Michelin**'s Choose Well — Live Well is a holistic, long-term strategy for changing how the company helps its employees, as well as their covered spouses and domestic partners, approach health. Supported by senior leaders, this program puts advocates in the center of everything to help people navigate the health care system. Programs are personalized, quantifiable, and linked to a fifteen-year ROI model. They integrate preventive care with healthy food choices, assessments, coaching, lifestyle and chronic condition management, and more.

- **PepsiCo** offers comprehensive programs to two hundred thousand employees and family members through Healthy Roads, a wellness program established in 2004. Available to all employees whether or not they enroll for medical coverage, the program promotes prevention and quality care. Its success is determined by decreased trends, increased healthy behaviors, and decreased health risks. In 2009, the company focused on weight management and obesity.

- The goal of Union Pacific Wellness is to make **Union Pacific** the healthiest company in the United States. The company's offerings have evolved since 1987 and continue to support healthy lifestyles and environments for more than forty-five thousand employees and spouses. The philosophy is, "Every step you take on the path of wellness leads to a richer, fuller life. Take charge, feel better, live more. And know you have Union Pacific's support." The program assesses and intervenes with eleven health risk factors, including asthma, blood pressure, cholesterol, depression, diabetes, physical inactivity, and other lifestyles.

In 2011, forty-eight companies won NBGH platinum awards. Nine consistently have won on the platinum level for five years since 2007: Baptist Health South Florida, Intel Corporation, Quest Diagnostics, Union Pacific, Campbell Soup Company, General Mills, Sprint, Target, and Unum. UPMC and UPMC Health Plan earned platinum status the last three consecutive years.

Two companies, American Express and Intel Corporation, won the new NBGH **Global Distinction Award** for developing programs so comprehensive that they cover all physical and psychosocial aspects of well-being and improve the productivity of employees and their dependents worldwide.

Remember that building an award-winning wellness and health management program is achieved much the same way an individual employee improves his health — with a vision, commitment, the right information, and the right interventions. Success is a matter of taking one step at a time, gaining support from others, and establishing goals that lead to big gains and wins.

SUCCESS GALLERY

Dave Goetzel

HEALTH ACHIEVEMENT:
LOST 151 POUNDS

EMPLOYER:
QUAD/GRAPHICS, WISCONSIN

JOB TITLE:
IT ENTERPRISE
NETWORKS MANAGER

At six feet one and 371 pounds, my BMI, or body mass index, was forty-nine and my medical chart described me as morbidly obese.

My weight loss journey started October 28, 2008, right after I saw my younger daughter push herself away from the table without clearing her plate simply because she was full. I was brought up to finish all of my dinner, so to see my daughter listen to her body and stop eating made a big impact on me.

I met with Pat Buck, a registered dietitian, who advised me to write down everything I ate over a two-week period. In those two weeks I lost five pounds because I adjusted myself to really think about what I was eating.

My wife, Karen, helped me continue the journey by planning healthier meals and serving smaller portions, and my daughters, Brittany and Becky, inspired me by their interest in diet and exercise.

My diet, aimed at consuming no more than two thousand calories a day, was more about cutting back on foods than cutting them out entirely. One big change was eating breakfast, which I'd always skipped, to get my metabolism going. Also, I always ate from a small plate and made smart substitutions, such as sugar-free popsicles instead of ice cream,1% milk, and spray butter.

I saved even more calories by switching to low-calorie beers and measured mixed drinks.

I also jog, lift weights, and use an elliptical machine to get more cardio exercise. After dinner and on weekends I stay active so I don't fall into the couch potato trap. As a result, my family now has a newly refinished basement.

Living in this way, I hit my goal of two hundred fifty pounds on October 15, 2009. As of December 9, 2009, I weighed 239 and have a new goal: 225 pounds. I feel ecstatic. It used to be that I could only buy clothes at Walmart. Now I can walk into Kohl's or American Eagle Outfitters and buy anything. I also can jog with my older daughter, who runs track.

I like telling my story to other participants in the Choose to Lose program at the Quad/Graphics Fitness Center. I tell people to remember that it takes time to lose weight. They didn't put it all on in a day or a week or a month. So they shouldn't expect it to come off that quickly.

BUILD YOUR BEST WELLNESS AND HEALTH MANAGEMENT PROGRAM

Answer these questions as they relate to your company:

1. Has your company investigated the opportunity to apply for wellness accreditation or engaged a vendor who has won national awards?

2. Do you think your company would be interested in online webinars to discuss how to apply for awards as well as consultations on how to achieve them?

3. Can you share with your colleagues the names and missions of organizations that offer awards and have scorecard templates available? Can you discuss why these factors may be important in your vendor selection?

4. Are you familiar with the Wellness Council of America and all the free, reliable, educational materials it offers for downloading?

5. Is your leadership and management team aware of the free white papers and research articles available to help you add novelty and fun elements to your program as well as improve its offerings and participation levels?

Chapter 11

LEADERS AS CHANGE AGENTS

Studies show management style and perception of management support are strong influencers on participation in employer-sponsored wellness and health productivity programs.

There's no disputing the success of Lincoln Industries in Nebraska which, under the leadership of Hank Orme since 1999, has grown 19% per year except for 2009 and 2010. The company, however, gained back in 2011 everything it had lost during those two recession years.

But growing revenue at least 15% annually is only one passion of the leader of this midsize manufacturing company, which specializes in products that require high-performance metal finishing. Orme also believes in developing people to their fullest potential. Every month his company measures progress on its business goals and its employees' wellness goals.

For five years, Lincoln Industries has been named one of the 25 Best Medium Companies to Work for in America. In November 2007, it won a national Innovation in Prevention Award from the U.S. Department of Health and Human Services for its efforts in promoting healthy lifestyles in the community.

The company's Go! Platinum wellness program, which won the distinguished C. Everett Koop National Health Award in 2008, offers quarterly physicals, risk assessments, stop smoking programs, educational seminars, and a year-long physical activity challenge. The program won, according to the Koop award, because of its metrics. Lincoln Industries achieved a 9.7% drop in health care costs from 2006 to 2007 and another dramatic drop — from 34% to 17% — in claims associated with lifestyle behaviors.

MOUNTAINEER PRESIDENT

In 2011 35% of Americans had three conditions that can raise their risk of cardiovascular disease, according to Orme, who added that only 19% of Lincoln Industries employees do. That is attributable to an on-site clinic with a physician assistant and full-time health coach available to help employees and their adult dependents achieve optimal well-being. Every year the dozens of employees who actually achieve their annual health goals are offered a platinum award — an all-expense paid trip to climb a 14,000-foot mountain in Colorado.

There at the base camp they'll find Orme, who has mastered yet another aspect of health and financial success: he models the desirable end results.

Orme works out at a gym with his wife six days a week. He lifts weights twice a week, and plays tennis singles as well as golf. His ultimate goal is to climb fifty 14,000-foot mountains. As of this writing, he is sixty-seven and has conquered twenty-four peaks. He plans to achieve his dream by the age of eighty. To learn more about how this leader creates such a positive culture, do visit www.lincolnindustries.com .

Success in the twenty-first century includes having a leader at every level of a company — from C-suite executives to the head of the smallest project team — who can adapt to a constantly changing market while nurturing a positive organizational culture that values people. Such leaders ensure the right employees display a personal commitment to achieve organizational results.

A white paper by Aon Hewitt[97] discusses the five pillars for building a performance culture and reinforces an important leadership message. The pillars are:

1. An environment empowering people to take accountability for the right results

2. Rewards that motivate them to contribute to sustainable success

3. Business practices that provide them with real opportunity for impact and growth

4. Climate of trust in which they feel valued, confident, and ready to give their best

5. Inspiring leadership that sets the right direction

An organization's culture of health is a matter of certain elements converging, according to Cheryl Larson, vice president of the Midwest Business Group on Health (MBGH), a nonprofit coalition of large, self-insured public and private companies.

"A good culture needs the right combination of senior leadership commitment and effective company benefit policies," Larson said. "It also needs a safe, inviting environment to encourage employees to take self-responsibility for their health."

Especially in difficult times, leaders and human resources departments must persuade employees to do things differently and to become more conscious of the role each of them plays in their company and the role their company plays in the world. Jack Tomayko, co-founder of The Tomayko Group who bought out his partners in 2004, likes his employees to have autonomy and enjoy their work with passion and purpose.

DISTRIBUTING THE WEALTH

When he took sole ownership of The Tomayko Group — a collection of integrated health care companies and services specializing in diagnostic imaging — he also found a way of ensuring his employees understand their direct impact on the company's success. All of them, no matter their positions or titles, equally share in the company's profit-sharing program. As of this writing, more than $1.3 million has been distributed to employees since Tomayko took over.

There are other ways The Tomayko Group has built a positive culture of health. Officially begun in 2008, its Travel to Good Health wellness program has conducted campaigns around physical activity, weight loss, and stress/well-being. Its metric results are proving employees are enthusiastic and actively engaged. In 2011 The Tomayko Group was voted one of the Best Small Companies to Work For and one of the Healthiest Employers in Western Pennsylvania. Do visit www. tomaykogroup.com .

One thing is for sure: no change occurs without a leader who believes the change has a positive purpose, communicates that purpose and its importance, and demonstrates the ability to capture employees' hearts and minds. **Studies show that management style and perception of management support are strong influences on participation in employer-sponsored health and wellness programs.**[98]

The Pittsburgh Business Group on Health (PBGH), an employer-led coalition that drives and delivers health care and benefits, points to an example. Over the past five years PBGH has introduced a number of ready-to-implement programs for employers. According to Christine Whipple, executive director, one such program was particularly well received.

"That company's CEO promoted the program through an introductory letter to employees, encouraged participation, and signed the letter," Whipple said. "Of all the employers that implemented the physical activity walking program, this employer had the most enrollees and the highest participation."

The outcome was fortunate, she added, since 17% of the employee population in the company took diabetes medication.

Another case in point surfaces at Aetna, where a positive, purposeful corporate culture and strong leadership manifests in employees using the very programs the insurance company offers its members.

"Many of the wellness and disease prevention programs available to Aetna customers started with Aetna's own employees," said Chairman, CEO and President Mark Bertolini, an early advocate for programs that emphasize health education, personal awareness, and individual action. Over the years Aetna's internal programs also have provided insight and impetus for other like-minded organizations.

SELF-EVALUATIONS FOR LEADERS

How do good, enlightened leaders evaluate how effective their own performance has been on a daily basis? Check out Partnership for Prevention's Leading by Example

Organizational Assessment Tool, though this checklist can help keep leaders on track:

- Did our team achieve the strategic goals established for each quarter and the year? Did we make a profit for our division, department, and stakeholders?

- Did we help recruit top talent, reduce turnover, and recognize and retain the most talented employees?

- Did we show an emotional heart in our dealings with staff, in addition to striving for a profit margin of 15% per year?

- Did our senior leadership team seek employees' input when instituting change?

- Did our team achieve a reduction in unscheduled leave time, disability and workers' compensation claims, and, if so, what were the total savings?

- Did we tie the bonuses we awarded and performance evaluations we wrote to how our directors engaged managers and others as they expanded the company's wellness and health management programs?

- Did we help facilitate and achieve within our company innovation and creative thinking with interdisciplinary teams?

- Did we model a positive health culture and encourage employees to thrive and achieve healthy, balanced quality lifestyles at work and home, and in the community?

- Did we, the management team, personally participate in the company's comprehensive, integrated wellness programs?

Jerry Noyce, president and CEO of Health Enhancement Research Organization (HERO), put it this way: "Leadership from the top of the organization sends a clear message that an employee health management program is important to our business strategy and should be taken seriously."

The next step, he added, is for department and unit heads to champion that program and help cement its message and make it real for all employees.

"The great thing about leadership commitment," Noyce said, "is it can be practiced by companies of all sizes, and is not limited to those with the most resources."

Below, in summary, is another checklist for the five major messages I have delivered in this book to keep organizations on track:

1. Good health is a good business strategy that requires understanding and applying the right information, right interventions, and right incentives at the right time.

2. Promoting optimal health and well-being involves education, policies, benefits, prosocial motivation, quality relationships, and cultural transformation.

3. Healthy employees enjoy a sense of well-being and are more productive, satisfied, engaged, and creative, which decreases a company's health costs both directly and indirectly and leads to a positive ROI.

4. A total health management program is a two-way agreement. Companies can implement a great program and provide multi-program components, education, incentives, and opportunity. But employees and their families also must be

responsible and take actionable steps to maintain or improve their health.

5. Creating healthy workplaces means using best practices for a bigger social good and forging partnerships with vendors, providers, government agencies, neighborhoods, schools, and hospitals.

An organization leading the way for such collaboration is the **National Priorities Partnership,**[99] which offers consultation support to the U.S. Department of Health and Human Services on setting national policies and quality strategy planning. Forty-eight member organizations help identify strategies for achieving better care, affordable care, healthy people, and healthy communities. They also work toward eliminating harm, waste and disparities. The **Robert Wood Johnson Foundation** is generously supporting the efforts of the partnership.

We now live in a world where most leaders, stakeholders, partners, and agencies would agree that success is not measured by profit margins alone, or by positions, titles, or awards. Success today includes contributing significantly to improving the health and well-being of all global citizens. Totally succeeding is the only way we all can rest comfortably in the knowledge we have good hearts.

SUCCESS GALLERY

Jennifer Harstad

HEALTH ACHIEVEMENT:
LOST 32 POUNDS AND
FOUR INCHES OFF HER
WAISTLINE

EMPLOYER:
BLUE CROSS AND BLUE
SHIELD OF MINNESOTA

JOB TITLE: NURSE

I used to work out frequently at the YMCA, but I found it difficult, as the kids got older, to fit in workouts between work and all their activities. I wasn't exercising at all, and I was noticing the effects — lack of energy, increased hunger, weight gain, and poor attitude.

When I heard about the extremely affordable classes that Blue Cross and Blue Shield was offering, I thought it was a great idea to attend. That doesn't mean that I ran right to my computer and signed up. I was nervous, scared, even concerned I would look silly or wouldn't be able to keep up with everyone else.

I signed up during the second week of a Zumba class and actually followed through and attended. I loved it and found there was no reason to fear going. Most people in the class were just like me. They were trying to find a fun form of exercise to fit into their busy schedules.

The instructors from BRX Fitness take the time to teach us what we need to know. They offer options throughout the class to increase or decrease the intensity of the workout, too. Frequently they even change the workouts so they never get old or boring. Most of all, they encourage us throughout the workout.

First I noticed my energy level increase. My head felt clearer at work and I felt an increased efficiency.

Next I noticed that I was starting to regain a positive attitude and that my appetite was decreasing. When I was hungry I made better choices.

I've lost thirty-two pounds in seven months, including the dreaded belly fat, and my waistline has decreased four inches. My blood pressure, which had been creeping up to the borderline hypertension range, is back down in the normal range now.

BUILD YOUR BEST WELLNESS
AND HEALTH MANAGEMENT PROGRAM

Answer these questions as they relate to your company:

1. Does your senior leadership team emphasize and reinforce with employees the core values of psychological safety, trust, respect, recognition, and autonomy? Are your leaders transparent, authentic, and compassionate?

2. Does your leadership team set defined employee expectations and annual strategic goals in addition to promoting a culture of health, mission, and vision?

3. Do your leaders ensure that employees have an opportunity to provide wellness support to others in addition to receiving support from others?

4. Can your leaders articulate to others how your company demonstrates and encourages meaning, passion, and motivation in the workplace and community?

5. How would your leaders rate their own knowledge, skill, and attitude with regard to demonstrating positive communications, positive relationships, and positive purpose to help your team and organization thrive?

Appendix A:
HEALTH MANAGEMENT ORGANIZATIONS

Agency for Healthcare Research and Quality (AHRQ) – As the health services research arm of the U.S. Department of Health and Human Services, this agency provides research and publications with evidence-based data written in English and Spanish.

American Association for Health Education (AAHE) – The association serves health educators and others who strive to promote the health of all people through education and other strategies. Among other functions, AAHE bridges the way between theory and research, offers technical assistance for drafting legislation, and assists in developing educational resources.

American College of Healthcare Executives (ACHE) – The college helps its members, who are all health care leaders, excel professionally and advance health care management. Members work in hospitals, health systems, clinics, universities, or similar settings.

American College of Occupational and Environmental Medicine (ACOEM) – Some fifty thousand physicians specializing in occupational and environmental medicine are represented by the college. It is the largest medical society dedicated to promoting the health of workers through preventive medicine, clinical care, disability management, research, and education.

American Institute for Preventive Medicine (AIPM) - Founded in 1983, the institute is an award-winning and internationally recognized authority on the development and implementation of programs and publications dealing with health promotion, wellness, medical self-care, and disease management. The institute sells more than one hundred fifty products and has helped more than thirteen million employees or members improve their health and well-being.

Corporate Health and Wellness Association (CHWA) - The first national nonprofit to focus on the health of employers, employees and their families, the association was founded on July 4, 2009 to grow the corporate wellness industry. Its birthday references Americans' independence from living unhealthy lifestyles.

Disability Management Employer Coalition (DMEC) - A nonprofit organization, the coalition helps companies minimize the impact of absence and disability. It provides tools, resources, and the latest research.

Gale Group Health and Wellness Database - This comprehensive periodical and reference database provides broad coverage in the areas of health, medicine, fitness, and nutrition. The Gale Group covers a diverse range of sources, including consumer health magazines, professional medical journals, and important referral information.

Health Enhancement Research Organization (HERO) – A national leader in the creation of employee health management, HERO teamed with Mercer Consulting to design a scorecard that allows employers to measure and evaluate their progress in six distinct categories for a maximum of 200 points. The scorecard, considered the gold standard, is offered as well as recommendations on how to continuously improve programs and services. HERO's 2010 annual report contains data on more than four hundred thirty employers of various sizes.

Health Promotion Advocates - Created in 2004, this nonprofit devotes itself to integrating health promotion concepts into national policy and elsewhere in society. It was instrumental in ensuring that prevention and wellness initiatives were included in the Health Care Reform Act.

Healthiest Employers - A privately held data research company, Healthiest Employers is focused on the corporate wellness industry. It provides a Web-based survey methodology that represents more than 2.5 million employees worldwide and seven hundred eleven employers.

Institute for Health and Productivity Management (IHPM) - A champion of the idea that healthy employees are a company's best competitive advantage in the world marketplace, IHPM helps employers integrate wellness with workers' comp, disability, leaves of absence, employee assistance programs, and more.

Integrated Benefits Institute (IBI) – The institute provides employers and their supplier partners with resources to establish the business value of health. It is a trusted source for benefits performance, analysis, practical solutions, and education.

International Association for Worksite Health Promotion (IAWHP) - An affiliate society to the American College of Sports Medicine, IAWHP is the first global association to support those who promote health at work sites. It provides access to educational and professional development resources and networking, supports local and regional efforts, and enables global collaboration and sharing.

International Foundation of Employee Benefit Plans (IFEBP) – This organization keeps compensation and benefits professionals current on the latest health industry developments. For more than thirty years, IFEBP has partnered with The Wharton School of the University of Pennsylvania to offer online programs and services.

International Positive Psychology Association (IPPA) – The mission of the association is to promote the science and practice of positive psychology as well as communication between researchers and others around the globe. It has three thousand members from more than seventy countries.

National Association of Health Underwriters (NAHU) - This organization promotes the business interests of those who sell health insurance services, including licensed health insurance agents, brokers, consultants, and benefits professionals who serve the health insurance needs of employers and individuals.

National Association of Insurance Commissioners (NAIC) - This organization represents more than four hundred thirty-four thousand insurance agents in the United States.

National Association of Manufacturers (NAM) – Eleven thousand manufacturing companies belong to the association, which has been an influential advocate for manufacturing since 1895. The association provides policies and health care reform information to its members.

National Business Group on Health (NBGH) – The voice for large employers on national health care issues, NBGH identifies, creates, and shares best practices in all matters related to health benefits, productivity, disability, and more. Its three hundred twenty-nine members provide health coverage for more than 55 million American workers and their families.

National Commission for Health Education Credentialing – The commission offers certification to health education specialists who meet certain standards and pass a national test.

National Commission for Quality Accreditation (NCQA) – The nation's major employers rely on NCQA accreditations to help them choose health plans, doctors, and other health care organizations to care for employees and their dependents.

National Wellness Institute (NWI) – One of the oldest wellness organizations in the country, the institute provides health promotion and wellness professionals the resources and services they need for professional and personal growth. This organization holds the popular and well-attended National Wellness Conference every year in Stevens Point, Wisconsin.

Society for Human Resource Management (SHRM) – With more than two hundred fifty thousand members and more than five hundred seventy-five affiliate chapters, the society is the world's largest association devoted to human resources management. It serves the interests of human resource professionals, offers resources and a national conference, and has more than two thousand product offerings. More than fifty percent of its members work in organizations with more than five hundred employees.

The Society for Public Health Education (SOPHE) – SOPHE promotes healthy communities, environments, and behaviors through its four thousand members, network of local chapters in twenty-five countries, and partnerships with other organizations.

U.S. Preventive Services Task Force (USPSTF) – An independent panel of primary care physicians, the task force reviews clinical preventive health services, such as screenings, counseling and medications, and develops recommendations for primary care clinicians and health systems.

Utilization Review Accreditation Commission (URAC) – This nationally sponsored organization promotes continuous improvement in the quality and efficiency of health care management through the process of accreditation, education, and measurements.

Wellness Council of America (WELCOA) - Established as a nonprofit in the 1980s, the council is among the most respected resources for workplace wellness in America. It provides free materials to non-members as well as its membership, which represents more than three thousand two hundred organizations.

World Health Organization (WHO) – The authority for health within the United Nations, WHO shapes the health research agenda and monitors and assesses health trends, among other functions. It defines health as a state of physical, mental and social well-being, and not as the absence of disease.

Appendix B:
WEBSITES, JOURNALS, AND CENTERS

NATIONAL SELECT SITES

Health.Data.Gov, http://www.data.gov/health

National Association for Health and Fitness-The Network of State and Governor's Councils
www.physicalfitness.org

National Business Group on Health
http://www.businessgrouphealth.org

National Cancer Institute, http://www.cancer.gov

National Center for Complementary and Alternative Medicine, http://nccam.nih.gov

National Center for Health Statistics,
http://www.cdc.gov/nchs/index.htm

National Coalition on Health Care, http://nchc.org

National Diabetes Information Clearinghouse (NDIC)
http://diabetes.niddk.nih.gov

National Health Association and the American Natural Hygiene Society, http://www.healthscience.org

National Health Information Center, www.health.gov/nhic

The National Institute for Occupational Safety and Health (NIOSH), www.cdc.gov/niosh

National Institute of Mental Health, www.nimh.nih.gov

National Institute on Aging, http://www.nia.nih.gov

National Institutes of Health, http://www.nih.gov

National Priorities Partnership
http://www.nationalprioritiespartnership.org

The National Weight Control Registry, http://www.nwcr.ws

National Wellness Institute
http://www.nationalwellness.org

GOVERNMENT SELECT SITES

CMS.gov, Centers for Medicare and Medicaid Services
http://www.cms.hhs.gov

Healthy People 2010-2020, http://www.healthypeople.gov

President's Council on Fitness, Sports & Nutrition
http://www.fitness.gov

U.S. Department of Health & Human Services
http://www.hhs.gov

U.S. Food and Drug Administration, http://www.fda.gov

U.S. Preventive Services Task Force
http://www.uspreventiveservicestaskforce.org

RESEARCH EMPHASIS SITES

Agency for Healthcare Research and Quality (AHRQ)
http://www.ahrq.gov

American College of Sports Medicine, http://www.acsm.org

American Heart Association, http://www.americanheart.org

American Psychological Association, http://apa.org

Center for Health Care Strategies, Inc. (CHCS)
http://www.chcs.org

Centers for Disease Control and Prevention
http://www.cdc.gov

The Commonwealth Fund
http://www.commonwealthfund.org

Diabetes Prevention Program, http://www.bsc.gwu.edu/dpp

Employee Assistance Professionals Association
http://www.eapassn.org

Employer Measures of Productivity, Absence and Quality
(EMPAQ), http://www.empaq.org

Health Affairs, http://www.healthaffairs.org

Health Enhancement Research Organization (HERO)
http://www.the-hero.org

The Henry J. Kaiser Family Foundation, http://www.kff.org

Institute for Health and Productivity Management
http://www.ihpm.org

Institute for Healthcare Improvement, http://www.ihi.org

Integrated Benefits Institute, http://www.ibiweb.org

International Association for Worksite Health Promotion
www.acsm-iawhp.org

International Foundation of Employee Benefit Plans
http://www.ifebp.org

International Positive Psychology Association
http://www.ippanetwork.org/

Lean Works! A Workplace Obesity Prevention Program
http://www.cdc.gov/leanworks

Mayo Clinic, http://www.mayoclinic.org

National Center for Biotechnology Information PubMed Clinical Queries, U.S. National Library of Medicine
http://www.ncbi.nlm.nih.gov/pubmed/clinical

National Collaborating Centre for Methods and Tools
http://www.nccmt.ca/eiph/index-eng.html

National Institute on Alcohol Abuse and Alcoholism
http://www.niaaa.nih.gov/Pages/default.aspx

National Institute on Drug Abuse
http://drugabuse.gov/drugpages/

National Quality Forum, http://www.qualityforum.org

Partnership for Prevention, http://www.prevent.org

WebMD, http://www.webmd.com

World Health Organization, http://www.who.int/en

SELECT PROFESSIONAL JOURNALS

American College of Sports Medicine Health & Fitness Journal
www.acsm-healthfitness.com

American Diabetes Association Journals
http://www.diabetesjournals.org

American Journal of Health Promotion
http://www.healthpromotionjournal.com

Applied Psychology: Health and Well-Being
http://www.wiley.com/bw/journal.asp?ref=1758-0846

Health Promotion Advocates, http://healthpromotionadvocates.org

Health Promotion International, http://heapro.oxfordjournals.org

International Association for Worksite Health Promotion, www.iawhp.org

Journal of Happiness Studies, http://www.springer.com/
social+sciences/well-being/journal/10902

Journal of Occupational Medicine and Toxicology
http://www.occup-med.com

The Journal of Positive Psychology
http://www.tandfonline.com/loi/rpos20

Journal of Workplace Behavioral Health, http://academic.research.
microsoft.com/Journal/16329/journal-of-workplace-
behavioral-health

The New England Journal of Medicine, http://www.nejm.org

SELECT CENTERS

Authentic Happiness-University of Pennsylvania
http://www.authentichappiness.com

Centre for Confidence and Well-Being-Scotland
http://www.centreforconfidence.co.uk

Families and Work Institute
http://www.familiesandwork.org

Gallup-Healthways Well-Being Index
http://well-beingindex.com

The Joint Commission, http://www.jointcommission.org

MeYou Health, http://www.meyouhealth.com

Positive Psychology Center-University of Pennsylvania
http://www.ppc.sas.upenn.edu

The Random Acts of Kindness Foundation
http://www.randomactsofkindness.org

The Resiliency Center, http://www.resiliencycenter.com

Sharecare, www.sharecare.com

SparkPeople, www.sparkpeople.com

Appendix C:

CHARTS ON WELLNESS PLANS AND STRATEGIES

• Aon Hewitt
• The Boston Consulting Group
• Buck
• Gallup
• Mercer
• Towers Watson
• Willis

CHWA •
HERO •
IAWHP •
IHPM •
IPPA •
NWI •
WELCOA •

Health Consulting Firms

Professional Wellness

Wellness Companies

Health Plans

• Bravo Wellness
• Health Enhancements
• Health Fitness
• HealthMedia
• Healthways
• Medifit
• RedBrick
• StayWell
• Virgin Miles
• WellSteps
• WorkPartners (UPMC)

Aetna •
American Health Care •
Blue Cross Blue Shield •
Cigna •
Humana •
United Behavioral Healthcare •
UPMC •

WELLNESS AND HEALTH PRODUCTIVITY
MULTI-YEAR STRATEGIES

YEAR 1 – TRADITIONAL	YEAR 2 – COMPREHENSIVE (EMPHASIZES LEADERSHIP)	YEAR 3 – INTEGRATIVE (EMPHASIZES CULTURE, ACCOUNTABILITY & INNOVATION)
• Announce vision and business rationale with senior leaders delivering the message	**Contains all components of Year 1 plus:**	**Contains all components of Year 2 plus:**
• Establish senior leadership planning and administrative processes	• Do biometric screening once every 3-5 years, as recommended	• Spell out leader and management roles, including necessary training
• Discuss benefits and compensation, with appropriate incentives	• Roll out multi-program components: online, telephonic, on-site, print, instant chat	• Tie in leader and management team bonuses and evaluations with engagement levels
• Emphasize a culture of health – how we live, work, learn, and play	• Sponsor health fair or event	• Create performance standards for active participation and support of wellness initiatives in all departments
• Combine safety and wellness committee meetings, if necessary	• Expand health coaching for all employees	
• Implement tools: – Employee interest survey – Health risk questionnaire (annual) – Biometric screenings (optional)	• Present Introduction to Absence Leave Management and integrated EAP	• Integrate EAP with disability and workers' compensation services, including cross referrals
	• Create on-site and/or online education webinars, webcasts, podcasts and videos	• Expand programs with other lifestyle components such as positive psychology
• Place health coach advocacy calls	• Leverage social media tools for campaigns, starting with a blog by content expert and FAQ	• Add new design models to increase behavior changes, e.g. BJ Fogg or AMSO
• Create Web-based portals and online lifestyle and chronic conditions management programs	• Create wellness committee and set up an annual operational plan as well as training of champions	• Create ongoing campaigns for all lifestyle behaviors
• Create nurse advice line, including instant chat	• Create incentive design plan based on progress and outcome	• Promote community events and guest speakers
• Create educational materials, including pdf files for downloading	• Choose one to two major campaign focuses, e.g., physical activity and/or weight management	• Increase engagement and quality outcomes; increase productivity, morale and retention; decrease turnover and health care costs
• Plan health fair (optional)	• Promote community events that engage families	• Integrate programs, metrics, and outcomes
• Promote community events		• Provide quarterly scorecard for site locations
• Provide marketing materials	• Evaluate outcomes with metrics – semiannual scorecards tracking reduction in risk factors with aggregate group data, and program satisfaction surveys	• Continuously improve products and programs using feedback from surveys, virtual focus groups and metrics on social media tools
• Distribute satisfaction survey – process and outcome measures		

Reprinted and adapted with permission from Chapman Institute

Acknowledgments

Family members, friends, professional colleagues, business associates, and clients have encouraged me to write this book. I am grateful not only for support but their feedback after hearing my presentations at national conferences and seminars. Their enthusiasm for the topics that drive me — health and wellness, positive psychology, work/life balance, innovation, and leadership — inspired me to follow through with writing.

I extend special thanks to my sisters, Mim Bizic and Alexandra Nolan, and their adult children, Nick and Angela, respectively, for ongoing support and constructive suggestions.

Lorraine Ash, my editor, deserves special appreciation. In addition to possessing awesome editorial skills, she is a fountain of positive energy and kindness.

I owe a debt of gratitude to Dave Weir, president of UPMC WorkPartners, and my colleagues Marie Sonnet, Sandy Carpenter, Madelyn Fernstrom, and Sandra Caffo for their initial interest and encouragement.

John Riedel and Gail Wagnild, researchers and independent senior consultants, provided insights which have been incalculable.

I thank the companies who won awards from the National Business Group on Health and others for permitting me to briefly describe their programs and present the personal testimonials of some of their employees. Their accomplishments serve as best practices and role models to help others improve individual and organizational health.

My gratitude also goes out to the Health Enhancement Research Organization for introducing me to leaders who graciously granted me phone interviews and email exchanges.

Lastly, I thank the World Health Organization for granting permission to include the global action health model chart in this book as well as the U.S. Department of Health and Human Services and the Office of the Surgeon General for their cooperation.

About the Author

Rose K. Gantner, EdD, senior director of health promotion, consumer education, training and innovation at the UPMC Health Plan in Pittsburgh, Pennsylvania, has thirty years of experience in wellness and counseling psychology. She has worked as CEO for two hospitals for Magellan Health Service and as vice president of managed care, employee assistance programs, and wellness at Corphealth. In addition to founding and directing her own counseling and psychology practice, Dr. Gantner has served as a health management consultant to state government agencies, private organizations, and commercial groups.

An accomplished speaker, she has taught clinical psychology and health education at three universities and presented at several national health care conferences. Dr. Gantner, who is listed in *World's Who's Who of Women*, also has published numerous articles on wellness and created a nine-part series of tapes on stress and motivation for American Learning Systems.

She received a citation from the U.S. Department of Defense for serving two tours in the Republic of South Vietnam for the American Red Cross as an executive program director. After her service abroad she earned her master's degree in Health Education from the University of Pittsburgh and her doctorate in Counseling Psychology from Auburn University.

Dr. Gantner is a member of the International Association for Worksite Health Promotion, International Positive Psychology Association, and the National Wellness Institute. She also is a diplomate member of the American College of Wellness.

NOTES

1   Morbidity and Mortality Weekly Report, *Occupational injuries and deaths among younger workers—United States, 1998-2007*, no. 15, 2010, 449.

2   Katherine Baicker, David Cutler and Zirui Song, "Workplace Wellness Programs Can Generate Savings," *Health Affairs*, vol. 29 (2010): 304-311.

3   "Chronic Disease Prevention and Health Promotion," *Centers for Disease Control and Prevention*, www.cdc.gov/chronicdisease/index.htm (accessed Jan. 2011).

4   "Bend the Healthcare Trend," *National Association of Health Underwriters*, http://www.nahueducationfoundation.org/books/books.cfm (accessed Nov. 10, 2011).

5   Gina Kolata, "Law May Do Little to Curb Unnecessary Care," *The New York Times*, Mar. 29, 2010, http://www.nytimes.com/2010/03/30/health/30use.html (accessed Jan. 2, 2011).

6   Dee Edington, *Zero Trends: Health as a Serious Economic Strategy* (Ann Arbor: University of Michigan Health Management Research Center, 2009), 20-22.

7   "The Future of Employee Wellness: Where Are We Headed?" *PricewaterhouseCooper's Trendsetter Barometer*, http://www.barometersurveys.com (accessed Oct. 13, 2010).

8   "Public Health's Inconvenient Truth: The Need to Create Partnerships With the Business Sector," *Preventing Chronic Disease*, http://www.cdc.gov/pcd/issues/2009/apr/08_0236.htm (accessed May 22, 2010).

9   U.S. Department of Health and Human Services. *A Report of the Surgeon General: How Tobacco Smoke Causes Disease: What It Means to You*, 2010, http://www.cdc.gov/tobacco/data_statistics/sgr/2010/consumer_booklet/pdfs/consumer.pdf .

10 U.S. Department of Health and Human Services, *Treating Tobacco Use and Dependence, Clinical Practical Guideline: 2009 Update*.

11 "Smoking Cessation: The Economic Benefits," *American Lung Association*, http://www.lungusa.org/press-room/press-releases/positive-roi-for-states.html (accessed 2010).

12   Nicko Pronk, et al., "Obesity Fitness, Willingness to Communicate Health Care Costs," *Medicine and Science in Sports Exercise*, vol. 31, no. 11 (1999): 1535-1543.

13   Cynthia Ogden, Molly Lamb, Margaret Carroll and Katherine Flegal, "Obesity and Socioeconomic Status in Adults: United States, 1988-1994 and 2005-2008," *NCHS Data Brief*, no. 50, http://www.cdc.gov/nchs/data/databriefs/db50.htm .

14   "Stress In The Workplace, Job Stress, Occupational Stress, Job Stress Questionnaire," *The American Institute of Stress*, http://www.stress.org/topic-workplace.htm (accessed 2010).

15   Jennifer Soong, "The Debt-Stress Connection," *WebMD*, Aug. 2008, http://www.webmd.com/balance/features/the-debt-stress-connection.

16   Daniel B. Nash, JoAnne Reifsnyder, Raymond J. Fabius, Valerie P. Pracilio, *Population Health: Creating a Culture of Wellness* (Burlington: Jones and Bartlett Publishing, 2011), 125.

17   "Enhancing Corporate Performance by Tackling Chronic Disease," *World Economic Forum Report,* http://www3.weforum.org/docs/WEF_HE_TacklingChronicDisease_Report_2010.pdf (accessed 2010).

18   "Chronic Disease Cost Calculator User Guide," *Centers for Disease Control and Prevention,* www.cdc.gov/nccdphp/resources/calculator.htm (accessed Dec. 2010).

19   "Blueprint for Health: A Framework for Total Cost Impact," *Human Capital Foundation and Riedel & Associates with the American College of Occupational and Environmental Medicine and the National Business Coalition on Health*, http://blueprint.acoem.org (accessed Dec. 2010).

20   Dee Edington, "Company Wellness Programs Pay Off Over Time," *Business News Daily*, Aug. 19, 2010, http://www.businessnewsdaily.com/company-wellness-program-pay-off-over-time-0465.

21   Towers Watson and the National Business Group on Health, "Survey: Employers Fret over Workers' Poor Health Habits," *The Wall Street Journal*, Feb. 22, 2010, http://blogs.wsj.com/health/2010/02/22/survey-employers-fret-over-with-workers-poor-health-habits.

22   Judd Robert Allen, "Achieving a Culture of Health: The Business Case," *Health Enhancement Systems white paper* (2010): 1-6.

23   Dee Edington, *Zero Trends: Health as a Serious Economic Strategy* (Ann Arbor: University of Michigan Health Management Research Center, 2009), 37.

24   "Patient Protection and Affordable Care Act," *Health Promotion Advocates*, http://healthpromotionadvocates.org/2011/06/affordable-

care-act (accessed Jun. 29, 2011).

25 "A Helping Hand for Small Businesses: Health Insurance Tax Credits," *Families USA and Small Business Majority*, http://www.familiesusa. org/assets/pdfs/health-reform/Helping-Small-Businesses.pdf (accessed Jul. 11, 2010).

26 Judd Robert Allen, "Achieving a Culture of Health: The Business Case," *Health Enhancement Systems white paper* (2010): 3.

27 Edgar H. Schein, *Organizational Culture and Leadership: 4th Edition* (San Francisco: Jossey-Bass, 2010).

28 Buck Consultants, *Working Well: A Global Survey of Health Promotion and Workplace Wellness Strategies*, Nov. 15, 2009, www.bucksurveys.com.

29 Isabel Diana Fernandez, "Association of Workplace Chronic and Acute Stressors With Employee Weight Status: Data From Worksites in Turmoil," *Journal of Occupational and Environmental Medicine*, no. 52 (Jan. 2010): 34-41.

30 Center for Work-Life Policy, www.worklifepolicy.org.

31 Tom Rath and Jim Harter, *Wellbeing: The Five Essential Elements* (New York: Gallup Press, 2010), 6.

32 Leave Absence Webinar, *Kronos, Inc.*, www.kronos.com (accessed Aug. 30, 2010).

33 Jody Heymann, Alison Earle and Jeffrey Hayes, "McGill Study: U.S. Protections for Working Families, Worst of all Affluent Countries," *McGill Newsroom*, Feb. 1, 2007, http://www.mcgill.ca/ newsroom/news/item/?item_id=23720.

34 Ilyse Schuman, "Work-Life Balance Award Act Fails," *Employment Law Update*, http://www.dcemploymentlawupdate.com/2010/06/articles/ workfamily-balance/worklife-balance-award-act-fails (posted Jun. 17, 2011).

35 "Moving Work Forward: Society for Human Resource Management and Families and Work Institute Launch Workplace Flexibility Partnership," *Families and Work Institute*, http://familiesandwork.org/ site/newsroom/movingworkforward-release.html (accessed May 11, 2011).

36 Psychologically Healthy Workplace Program, *American Psychological Association*, www.phwa.org (accessed Mar. 2011).

37 Abhijeet Rane, et al., *The Future of Workplaces*, http://livingworkplace. skype.com/assets/pdf/Future_of_Workplaces-GigaOmPRO.pdf (accessed Mar. 2011).

38 BJ Fogg, "The Behavior Grid: 35 Ways Behavior Can Change," *Stanford University*, http://www.bjfogg.com/fbg_files/page7_1.pdf (accessed Apr. 29, 2011).

39   Kevin Oschner, "The Formation of Habit: Report form the NeuroLeadership Summit," *Leadership Channel* podcast, Nov. 3, 2010, http://www.totalpicture.com/shows/leadership/social-cognitive-neuroscience-and-leadership-a-podcast-with-kevin-ochsner.html .

40   Kelly Traver and Betty Kelly Sargent, *The Program: The Brain-Smart Approach to the Healthiest You. The Life-Changing 12-Week Method* (New York: Atria Books, 2009), 31.

41   Michael O'Donnell, "Changing Behaviors," *WELCOA's News and Views, 3rd edition* (2010), http://www.welcoa.org/freeresources/pdf/newsviews_odonnell.pdf.

42   Omar Shafey, Michael Eriksen, Hana Ross and Judith Mackay, *The Tobacco Atlas, Third Edition* (Georgia: American Cancer Society, 2009).

43   "Smokefree Laws and Policies," *American Lung Association,* http://www.lungusa2.org/slati/smokefree_laws.php (accessed Feb. 5, 2010).

44   U.S. Department of Health and Human Services, *Clinical Practice Guideline for Treating Tobacco Use and Dependence: 2008 Update.*

45   John Riedel, Cyndy Nayer, "Value-Based Design: A New Powerful Perspective for Worksite Health Promotion," *The Art of Health Promotion* (Mar./Apr. 2010), http://www.vbhealth.org/wp-content/uploads/AHP-HPP-primer-3.2010.pdf.

46   Buck Consultants, *Working Well: A Global Survey of Health Promotion and Workplace Wellness Strategies,* Nov. 2010, www.bucksurveys.com.

47   "The Biology of Emotion – And What It May Teach Us About Helping People to Live Longer," *Harvard School of Public Health, Harvard Public Health Review,* http://www.hsph.harvard.edu/news/hphr/chronic-disease-prevention/happiness-stress-heart-disease (accessed Aug. 25, 2011).

48   Martin Seligman, *Authentic Happiness: Using The New Positive Psychology to Realize Your Potential for Lasting Fulfillment* (New York: The Free Press, 2002), 46-61.

49   Barbara Fredrickson, *Positivity: Top-Notch Research Reveals the 3-to-1 Ratio That Will Change Your Life* (New York: Three Rivers Press, 2009), 32.

50   Kim Cameron, *Positive Leadership: Strategies for Extraordinary Performance* (San Francisco: Berrett-Koehler Publishers, Inc., 2008), 3.

51   Alex Linley, Susan Harrington and Nicola Garcea, *Oxford Handbook of Positive Psychology and Work* (New York: Oxford University Press, Inc., 2010), 3.

52   Wayne Baker, Rob Cross and Melissa Wooten, "Positive Organizational Network Analysis and Emerging Relationships," in *Positive Organizational Scholarship: Foundations of a New Discipline,* eds. Kim S. Cameron, Jane E. Dutton and Robert E. Quinn. (San Francisco:

Berrett-Koehler, 2003), 325-342.

53 "Productivity Suffers in Negative Workplaces," *Right Management, ManpowerGroup*, http://www.right.com/news-and-events/press-releases/2010-press-releases/item20355.aspx (accessed Nov. 2010).

54 "Majority of American Workers Not Engaged in Their Jobs," *Gallup*, http://www.gallup.com/poll/150383/majority-american-workers-not-engaged-jobs.aspx (accessed Oct. 2011).

55 William Macey and Benjamin Schneider, "The Meaning of Employee Engagement," *Industrial and Organizational Psychology*, no. 1 (2008): 3-30, http://onlinelibrary.wiley.com/doi/10.1111/j.1754-9434.2007.0002.x/abstract.

56 "Study Reveals Characteristics of Disengaged Workers," *Society for Human Resource Management*, http://www.shrm.org/hrdisciplines/employeerelations/articles/Pages/CharacteristicsofDisengaged.aspx (accessed Oct. 15, 2010).

57 "Disengagement Can Be Really Depressing," *Gallup*, http://gmj.gallup.com/content/127100/disengagement-really-depressing.aspx (accessed Sept. 4, 2010).

58 Roy Spence, *It's Not What You Sell, It's What You Stand For: Why Every Extraordinary Business Is Driven by Purpose* (New York: Penguin, 2009), 10-12.

59 "Productivity Suffers in Negative Workplaces," *Right Management, ManpowerGroup*, http://www.right.com/news-and-events/press-releases/2010-press-releases/item20355.aspx (accessed Nov. 2010).

60 "Fortune's 100 Best Companies to Work For," *Great Places to Work Institute*, http://www.greatplacetowork.com (accessed Dec. 2010).

61 Nicholas Christakis and James Fowler, *Connected: The Surprising Power of Our Social Networks and How they Shape Our Lives* (New York: Little Brown and Company, 2009), 37.

62 Bill Hendrick, "iPods, Texting at 100: How Centenarians Stay Hip: Eating Healthfully, Staying Active and Socially Connected Among Secrets of 100-Year-Olds," *WebMD*, May 7, 2010, http://www.webmd.com/healthy-aging/news/20100507/ipods-texting-at-100-how-centenarians-stay-hip.

63 David Snowdon, Lydia Greiner, Susan Kemper, N. Nanahakkara and J. Mortimer, "Linguistic Ability in Early Life and Longevity: Findings from the Nun Study," in *The Paradoxes of Longevity*, ed. J.-M. Robine. (New York: Springer, 1999), 103-113.

64 Ronald D. Siegle and Steven M. Allison, "Positive Psychology: Harnessing the Power of Happiness, Mindfulness, and Personal Strength," *Harvard Health Publications* (2011): 1-37.

65 National Association of Manufacturers, http://www.nam.org/Issues/
    Official-Policy-Positions/Human-Resources-Policy/HRP-02-
    Health-Policy.aspx (accessed Sept. 20, 2010).

66 "2005 Absence Management Survey," *JHA and EBN Report*, http://www.
    edwardgroup.net/images/2005%20Absence%20Management%20
    Report.pdf (accessed Apr. 20, 2011).

67 "The WellSteps Performance Guarantee," *Wellsteps*, http://www.
    wellsteps.com//wellsteps-performance-guarantee
    (accessed Nov. 8, 2010).

68 James Canton, *The Extreme Future: The Top Trends That Will Reshape The World*
    (New York: Penguin Group USA, 2007), 57, 332.

69 David Croslin, *Innovate The Future: A Radical New Approach to IT Innovation*
    (New Jersey: Prentice Hall, 2010), 28.

70 "Specialized Incubators will Spur Middle East Innovation," *Blogging
    Innovation*, http://www.business-strategy-innovation.com/labels/
    Kamal%20Hassan.html (accessed 2010).

71 Braden Kelley, *Stoking Your Innovation Bonfire: A Road Map to a Sustainable
    Culture of Ingenuity and Purpose* (New Jersey: John Wiley & Sons, Inc.,
    2010).

72 Agency for Healthcare Research and Quality, http://www.ahrq.gov
    (accessed May 2011).

73 Stephanie Strom, "A $400 Million Gift to Genetic Institute,"
    The New York Times, Sept. 4, 2008.

74 Princeton Longevity Center, http://www.theplc.net
    (accessed May 2011).

75 Humana Inc., http://www.humana.com (accessed May 2011).

76 Michael Feuer, Max-Wellness, www.max-wellness.com
    (accessed May 2011).

77 "Social Media Shown to Sustain Participation in Online
    Health Programs," *iHealth Beat*, http://www.ihealthbeat.org/
    articles/2010/12/9/social-media-shown-to-sustain-participation-
    in-online-health-programs.aspx (accessed 2011).

78 "Internet Usage Statistics: The Internet Big Picture," *Internet World
    Stats, Usage and Population Statistics*, http://www.internetworldstats.com/
    stats.htm (accessed May 17, 2011).

79 "Older Adults and Social Media," *Pew Internet*, http://www.
    pewinternet.org/reports/2010/older-adults-and-social-media/
    report.aspx (accessed Aug. 15, 2011).

80 Ibid.

81 Brian Solis, *Engage! The Complete Guide for Brands and Business to Build,
    Cultivate, and Measure Success in the New Web* (New Jersey: John Wiley &

Sons, Inc., 2010), 13.

82   Benz Communications, www.benzcommunications.com (accessed
      May 17, 2011).

83   Brian Dolan, "Mobile Health Report, Fourth Quarter Review,"
      MobiHealthNews, Jan. 13, 2010.

84   Ibid.

85   "CSC's Leading Edge Forum: Disruptive Technologies to Reshape
      Delivery of Healthcare," *News Medical*, http://www.news-medical.
      net/news/20101207/CSCs-Leading-Edge-Forum-Disruptive-
      technologies-to-reshape-delivery-of-healthcare.aspx
      (accessed Dec. 7, 2010).

86   National Committee for Quality Assurance, www.ncqa.com.

87   Utilization Review Accreditation Commission, www.urac.org.

88   American Heart Association, www.americanheart.org.

89   American College of Occupational and Environmental Medicine,
      www.acoem.org.

90   American Psychological Association, www.apa.org.

91   Health Leaders Media, www.topleadershipteams.net.

92   Employee Assistance Society of America, www.easna.org.

93   Wellness Council of America, www.wellworkplaceaward.org.

94   C. Everett Koop National Award, www.thehealthproject.com.

95   Institute for Health Productivity Management, www.ihpm.org.

96   National Business Group on Health, www.businessgrouphealth.org.

97   Aon-Hewitt Consultants, *Pillars Required for Building a Performance Culture*,
      2010.

98   Kim Witte, "Managerial Style and Health Promotion Program,"
      Social Science & Medicine, no. 36 (1993): 227-235.

99   "National Priorities and Goals: Aligning Our Efforts to Transform
      America's Healthcare," *National Quality Forum* (2008), http://www.
      nationalprioritiespartnership.org/uploadedFiles/NPP/08-253-
      NQF%20ReportLo%5B6%5D.pdf (accessed May 2011).

Made in the USA
Charleston, SC
02 February 2013